'Beautiful autobiography of a talented player. What a great lesson that courage and hard work can make your dreams come true, even if it is not always easy to achieve.'

'You cannot put the book down once you start. Superb!'

'I didn't read it, I devoured it! A path full of pitfalls with success at the end.'

'Fascinating book, if you're passionate about football, I would recommend it.'

'Discover the character and personal story of a true champion. Perfect for football fans.'

'I was pleasantly surprised by this book. I was already a fan of Antoine Griezmann but there are a lot of stories in the book that endear me to him further, especially about his childhood and his difficulty making it in France.'

Reviews from Amazon.fr

ANTOINE GRIEZMANN

ANTOINE GRIEZMANN

My Autobiography

Reach Sport

30°

Inside cover images:

Inside front cover: 1998. The boy.

I was weaned on football.
This is our neighbourhood party – and my way of celebrating our victory in the World Cup.

Inside back cover: 2018. The man.

Sealed with a kiss.
The journey comes full circle as I celebrate being a part of the 2018 World Cup triumph in Russia.

With this book, I wanted to show how much I've struggled, but how I'm reaping the benefits from it today. It took a lot of tears to get here.

Antoine Griezmann

Reach Sport

www.reachsport.com

Written with Arnaud Ramsay.
Translation and updated content by Ric George.

'Derrière Le Sourire' originally published in 2017.

Published in Great Britain and Ireland in 2019 by
Reach Sport, a Reach PLC business,
5 St Paul's Square, Liverpool, L3 9SJ.

www.reachsport.com@SportMediaTM

Reach Sport is a part of Reach plc.
One Canada Square, Canary Wharf, London, E15 5AP.

1

Paperback ISBN: 978-1-911613-35-0
eBook ISBN: 78-1-911613-36-7

Photographic acknowledgements:
Antoine Griezmann, c/o Éditions Robert Laffont.
PA Images.

Design and typesetting by Reach Sport.

Printed and bound by CPI Group (UK) Ltd,
Croydon, CR0 4YY.

Contents

About The Translator:

This English language edition of Antoine Griezmann's autobiography has been translated by Ric George. While working as a sports journalist in Liverpool for 20 years, Ric was also a long-standing correspondent for 'France Football', and appeared as a pundit on the Canal Plus programme 'Les Specialistes, Premier League' from 2012-2014. He lives in Tours.

Introduction

RISE OF THE LITTLE PRINCE

Despite his diminutive stature, Antoine Griezmann is a football giant. Standing "somewhere between 5'7½" and 5'8" small, he overcame the obstacles which threatened to shatter his boyhood dream to scale the heights of the sport, conquering the world with the French national team in 2018.

It was a triumph which he hoped, and which many observers in France believed, would subsequently earn him football's greatest personal accolade: the coveted FIFA Ballon d'Or. Shortly before its original 2017 publication in the country of his birth, this autobiography expresses his joy at being voted third in that year's rankings, despite his suffering quick-fire losses the summer before in the Champions League final with Atlético Madrid and the European Championship final with France.

However, Atlético's Europa League victory over Marseille,

followed by France's World Cup success against Croatia in Russia, not to mention Atlético's defeat of Real Madrid to secure the European Super Cup, had made him a prime contender for the 2018 Ballon d'Or.

Before the ceremony in Paris, Griezmann admitted he hoped a French player would be able to end a decade of dominance by Cristiano Ronaldo and Lionel Messi. "It would be a shame if a Frenchman doesn't win it," he declared. "Maybe the Champions League is more important than the World Cup, but we will see."

According to the jury of journalists, that was so, Real Madrid's Croatian midfielder Luka Modrić finishing in first place, with Ronaldo second and Antoine again third, much to the surprise, and even disgust, of many compatriots.

Éric Olhats, the man who had spotted Griezmann's potential as a youngster and who took him to Real Sociedad before becoming his sporting adviser, knew how much the Ballon d'Or meant to him. "That's a tough blow for Antoine," he said. "What more could he have done to win a global competition? It's not totally outrageous for Modrić to finish ahead of him, but Cristiano on the other hand..."

Griezmann tried hard to hide his disappointment. "When I found out, you didn't want to be at home with me for the first two days!" he joked. "I am very proud of my year. There was a bit of disappointment when I heard the top three. But it's great to be on the podium and to be a World Champion. I'm on the right track (to win the Ballon d'Or).

"I have been on the podium twice, so I've got to carry on that way. He (Modrić) has had a great year, a great season. He won the Champions League and took Croatia far in the World Cup. It's journalists who voted and, for them, he deserved it.

I'm relying on my team-mates at my club and in the national team to be in Luka's place in the future."

The Atlético Madrid star had arguably been Europe's most consistent performer that year, registering 36 goals in all competitions, including in the semi-final and final of the Europa League – a competition in which he was voted the top player. Not only did he win the World Cup, he did so by making a significant contribution to France's success. He became the first man since 1986 to be involved in at least one goal in the round of 16, the quarter-final, semi-final and final. His penalty against Croatia in Moscow's Luzhniki Stadium took his tally to four, and he was awarded the Bronze Ball for being the tournament's third best player.

Antoine was widely quoted as saying he didn't know what else he had to do to claim the Ballon d'Or, a remark which was interpreted as arrogant. But it's a remark he didn't actually make. When interviewed during the ceremony, the point was put to him that he had scored in a World Cup round of 16, quarter final, and final, and made assists in the quarters and semis. "What more do you have to do?" he was asked. "Individually I don't know. From a collective point of view I won the Europa League, Super Cup and World Cup. It's thanks to my team-mates I'm here. I'm very happy to have these people in the France team and in my club."

There is a school of thought that if Antoine had played for Real Madrid rather than the less fashionable Atlético, then the Golden Ball would currently occupy pride of place on his mantelpiece.

It's a theory to which ex-Atlético striker Paulo Futre subscribes. The former Portugal international, who finished second behind Ruud Gullit in the 1987 voting, said on Twitter:

"Don't worry Griezmann. Sometimes winning the Champions League isn't even an historic thing. Maybe the problem is the colour of your team. Forza Atléti. A big hug for you superstar."

Not surprisingly, Atlético felt an injustice had been done. "It's much harder playing at Atlético than anywhere else because our history has always been based on work and doubling our efforts in order for us to challenge," coach Diego Simeone said. "As for Griezmann, I'm repeating what he said. If I were in his place I'd be pleased by what happened this year. He's been a World Cup winner, and that's very hard to do. After that, everyone can decide or choose what seems right for them. I want to congratulate Modrić, because he had a great season. But for me the best were (Raphaël) Varane and Griezmann."

Simeone's words were echoed by Antoine's Atlético team-mate, Antonio Adán. "He deserved it," he said. "He had a fantastic year and he was instrumental in winning trophies. It's a shame, but I can see him being confident about continuing to work, and the time will come where he wins. He knows that the event is gone and that he now has to look forward. He is young, he's at a big club and he has what it takes to win it."

Griezmann's route to the top has been circuitous, and as unconventional as admirable. After countless rejections in France, where size triumphed over skill, few may have pursued their dream of turning professional. However, even fewer would have left home to do it, particularly when it meant moving abroad. Especially at thirteen!

Éric Olhats, then a scout for Real Sociedad, succeeded where others had failed by recognising that Antoine's talent more than compensated for his lack of inches. "He cried at my place when he missed his family, to whom he is extremely close," revealed Olhats. “Neither they nor he realised the upheavals which would occur. When he returned to Bayonne after a weekend in Mâcon, his father had tears in his eyes, his mother would hide away and he wasn't good in himself. I paid his air fare so he could go back home. On the weekends that he stayed I would take him to games in Toulouse or Bordeaux, which I'd be watching for Real Sociedad. Even though he is not my son, I shared his joys and his sorrows.”

Over the years, and through the tears, such was Griezmann's determination to succeed that he shifted through Real's ranks to become the fans' favourite, a status he now holds in the Atlético and France teams.

“Antoine Griezmann's pride is mainly in being a complete player, possessing the full range of skills,” writes French journalist Arnaud Ramsay, who collaborated with Griezmann on this book originally titled *Derriére Le Sourire* (‘Behind The Smile’), which became a sporting best-seller in France. “He is as much of a goal scorer as a goal maker, he moves intelligently, is a clinical finisher, he tracks back, takes free-kicks and corners, is good with his head and with the right foot as much as the left. In short, he plays fair and gives his all. Another famous Atlético Madrid striker, the Spanish international Francisco Narváez – better known as Kiko – who won the League and Cup in 1996, summed him up thus: ‘He's a different kind of footballer, with a body made of iron and a foot made of silk.’”

How ironic that Griezmann owes his popularity in France to his years spent in Spain, a country which has brought him trophies, stardom and a wife. He was France's favourite footballer, their pin-up boy, even before he had won the World Cup; a player to whom youngsters can relate, with his Fortnite and Drake goal celebrations as well as a series of children's football books. And yet so little is known about him. "He is France's new Little Prince," adds Ramsay. "The likeness springs to mind because he bears the same first name as Antoine de Saint-Exupéry and sports, tattooed on his forearm, a quote from the writer/aviator which he uses as a mantra: *'Make your life a dream, and a dream, a reality.'*

"His popularity is there for all to see. His freshness, his spontaneity, his joie de vivre, his angelic face, his effectiveness on the field, his vision, the way he oozes football through all the pores of his skin, captivate the general public in France."

Griezmann's mischevious sense of humour has also caught the imagination. Ramsay explains: "He always gives (his wife) Erika dedications, even if it means picking up a fine.

"One time he dedicated his first goal against Valencia to her by lifting up his red and white shirt to reveal 'Feliz Cumple, Gordita!' ('Happy Birthday, Chubby!') followed by a heart sign. The following week the Spanish FA disciplinary committee hit him with a fine and issued him with a yellow card.

"As someone who is usually measured in his words, he shrugged off his reserved persona and muscled-up his game by sending an angry tweet: 'A fine and booking for congratulating my wife and this three days after… #GetOnWithOtherThings.'"

Griezmann is also popular with team-mates and, if his social media is anything to go by, a playful presence in the dressing room. Griezmann confessed to *L'Équipe* that he had to avoid eye contact with close friend Paul Pogba during Pogba's now-famous dressing room speech to the France team before the World Cup final against Croatia.

The Manchester United midfielder's inspirational address to his team-mates ended up going viral and Griezmann was impressed but he added: "Every time he speaks, I want to laugh! Paul is so used to 'disconnecting' that he surprised me. That's why, when he spoke, he never looked at me. He knew I'd have a little smile and could laugh at any moment. But it's good for him and for us too."

There are plenty of other tongue-in-cheek moments to recount, such as the time he posted an image on Instagram after Atlético's Super Cup triumph over city rivals Real Madrid. With Griezmann dressed in the robes of a king, it depicted Real's Sergio Ramos about to place a crown on his head. It all goes to show that life is never dull when Antoine is around.

The French language autobiography recounted Griezmann's career up to 2016/2017, but this edition completes the story and, indeed, Griezmann's remarkable journey to the summit of world football.

In a foreword to the original book, it's clear that Griezmann values his privacy but used this book to open up and give fans a rare inside track on the life of an international football superstar. Writer Ramsay paints the picture of how the process unfolded:

> *Four months of writing sessions produced what you are now holding in your hands. In front of the Dictaphone, Antoine spoke openly and bluntly, revealing an impressive memory of all his games and not going off on tangents.*
>
> *He was an eloquent speaker, even surprising his sister Maud, and Erika with his unfamiliar openness. He goes straight to the point and never strays.*
>
> *His daughter Mia, sucking her dummy, plucks up the*

courage from time to time by coming into the lounge for a cuddle from Dad. Hooki his French bulldog lets out a few impatient growls, eager to go into the garden, while Maud, lurking in the shadows, is an assuring presence.

In Spanish, which he uses more than his French, he is able to ask: "How do you say that again in French?" Antoine Griezmann, sticking to the game, also e-mailed me things he wrote, snippets of his life or scrapbooks, ranging from his transfer to Atlético to the birth of his daughter, via the moment where he learned that he would be in the top three for the Ballon d'Or.

The full life tour was completed by discussions with Éric Olhats, his sporting adviser and the man who brought him to Real Sociedad plus a visit to the family in Mâcon. It's there where his roots are planted, where his parents, Alain and Isabelle, became his perennial defenders, with younger brother Théo. Because the Griezmanns are above all a family affair.

It's been a long and winding road to the top that should serve as inspiration to young footballers. Aside from his rejection at an early age, Griezmann had to surmount a 13-month international ban for breaking a curfew with the France Under-21s and prove himself as a central striker in order to cement a place in the senior side.

Antoine opens up about his passion for South American culture, talks about his friendship with Paul Pogba and reveals why David Beckham is his all-time hero. He explains how close he came to signing for Tottenham and Arsenal and speaks honestly about the regular rumours linking him with a big money move to Manchester United. And he provides a fascinating glimpse into the characters of the two managers who have helped get the best out of him: Diego Simeone at Atlético Madrid and World Cup-winning France boss Didier Deschamps. There are insights and observations, too, on many famous names from the game, from Cristiano Ronaldo to Kylian Mbappé.

Ultimately, his story is a testimony that determination, dedication and drive will ultimately pay dividends. And, of course, that size doesn't matter.

1

DINING AT THE TOP TABLE

They say that just before you die you see your life flash in front of you. Don't worry, I'm in no hurry to experience this. But I have already had a glimpse of my life in fast-forward mode.

It is December 2016. My sister Maud, who looks after my press relations, calls me to firm up the details of an interview which was scheduled for two days later. *France Football* magazine is to present me with the French Player of the Year trophy *(1)*. It's voted for by previous winners, from Zinedine Zidane to Raymond Kopa *(2)*, from Thierry Henry to Jean-Pierre Papin, from Michel Platini to Karim Benzema. And I'm guessing she's trying to contact me to tell me how long the interview is going to last and where it will take place.

I've just finished training when I notice she's tried to reach me three times. That's very unusual for her. Often Maud is happy enough just to leave me a message telling me the necessary information so that I can get myself organised. This time, though, there is no message but there were three calls in a short space of time. That's odd. But there's no reason to panic or to change my routine. So after the session I'm sipping my yerba maté *(3)* through the bambilla from the calabash gourd with my South American team-mates at Atlético Madrid; Diego Godín, José María Giménez, Nicolás Gaitán and Angel Correa.

I finish things off by taking a hot bath for three minutes, followed by an eight-minute long, cold one. This helps me recover after training. Then I go for a shower.

Even though I don't change anything about my routine, I'm not totally comfortable with things. In a corner of my head these phonecalls have been bugging me. I shower more quickly than usual, I get dressed and then I leave.

"Hasta mañana, amigos."*(4)*

I climb into the car and get away from the training ground and I call Maud. While the phone is ringing a few questions are spinning around in my head. What's up with her? Has anything in particular happened?

Maud answers the phone and starts the conversation with a question: "You okay, *Toinou*?" Phew! I'm reassured now. When she calls me *Toinou* it's a good sign. It means everything is fine.

She then comes out with a classic: "On Thursday you've got a meeting at 2pm at the hotel AC La Finca." Perfect. That was the plan. That hotel, situated in a suburb of Madrid, has a nice, relaxed vibe and is not far from my home. Before she hangs up, Maud wants to tell me something. "You've got to keep this a secret. No-one must know," she says firmly. The next bit is a more confusing. "You are…" When Maud finishes her sentence my heart is beating like never before.

My mind goes blank. I don't know what to think. Half a second later she says again "You are…"

The sentence is short. However, it was as if Maud had deliberately withheld the suspense for five whole minutes. Finally, my mind is all over the place and I can only hear the end of what she wanted to tell me, which brought about an amazing:

"You are …ird!"

"What did you say?"

And Maud shouts: "You are third in the Ballon d'Or!"

I explode: "Yeeeessssss! F***, how great is that! I've made it, in the top three!"

The joy is huge. I am in my car. I'm screaming, I'm shouting. The people around me must be wondering what's going on. Right now I really don't care. I've got to take stock of what's happening to me, and how far I've come.

I, Antoine Griezmann, 25 years old, from Mâcon, who was rejected throughout France because of my size, am now among the top three players in the world!

Ever since my 14th year, living in Bayonne and being developed as a footballer by Real Sociedad, I suffered from being separated from my family. There was the new language – Spanish – to learn and to use with my team-mates, the tribulations of being a substitute, of having to warm up for the whole of the second half only never to come on, the bad periods in front of goal, the defeats, my two lost finals in the space of a few weeks in the Champions League and then in the Euros.

It's the life of a footballer whose many sacrifices have finally paid off. I think back to all the efforts I made, those afternoons working hard in training. All these efforts which have enabled me to become the third best player in the world *(5)*. That's the calendar year, not just the season. I am aware that this is just the beginning, that people will expect greater and greater things from me. But I feel I can handle all that. I reckon I haven't reached my full potential. It's important that I keep working day after day, to always give my team-mates everything.

I want my parents, my sister and my brother to be proud of me and little Mia to be proud of her dad. I want Erika to think "yes, that's my man and I'm proud of him," my mates to be able to say to themselves: "that's our Grizi," and that my *TeamGrizi* will be proud of me. But above all that it's important I make sure I keep enjoying my football. Basically, the road ahead is still long and there are a lot of things which will happen along the way. But I'm on the right track...

And so I join a select group, that of the prestigious Ballon d'Or, created by *France Football* in 1956 and which was only voted for by specialist journalists. Later the captains and the coaches of national teams were added to the jury under the auspices of FIFA. *France Football* has since reclaimed its property and gone back to the original format, so for this particular edition, it's the votes of 173 international journalists which have counted.

In the end, Cristiano Ronaldo leads with 745 points, well ahead of Lionel Messi, who has 316 points. I make up the trio with 198 points.

Seven juries have even put me as their first choice, those from the Czech Republic, the Caribbean island of Aruba, Libya, Lichtenstein, New Caledonia, Palestine and Swaziland! This is Ronaldo's fourth Ballon d'Or. At the time of writing Messi has five, which is a record. I am the 11th French player to come in the top three *(6)* and only the fourth to do so in 20 years. I definitely have a reason to feel satisfied, especially as I am not an out-and-out number nine. I don't consider myself to be a player who has to score every weekend. I place a greater importance on the collective side of things. I am all-round player. I don't just feel the need to attack.

Looking back, when it came to personal honours, 2016 turned out to be a rich year for me: I was named the best player at the Euros *(7)* by a jury of experts from UEFA, which included Sir Alex Ferguson and I was the tournament's top scorer with six goals. I was also the top footballer in La Liga thanks to my 22 goals and five assists in 38 games as well as being voted the fans' favourite player. Lastly I was named France's best overseas player by the Union National des Footballeurs Professionnnels (UNFP) *(8)*.

In the Ballon d'Or voting I find myself behind two players who are out of this world, two legends who, since 2008, have snapped up every individual honour between them. I am by no means questioning their talent, but we don't all have their marketing power. Messi and Ronaldo are above the rest. But in my view some other players would nevertheless have deserved as much. I'm thinking, for example, of Xavi or Andrés Iniesta after the 2010 World Cup, Gianluigi Buffon and Franck Ribéry.

In 2013, Ribéry had been so impressive with Bayern Munich, who won the Champions League, the Bundesliga and the German Cup. Franck only finished third in the Ballon d'Or.

That was such a shame because it would have been perfectly logical for him to have claimed the award. I understand how disappointed he was, because he had been the favourite to win it. There is no doubt that this came like a blow to the back of his head. The Ballon d'Or is still something magical, but it has lost a little of its attraction, its clout. Nevertheless I hope that one day I will be able to achieve this accolade. But it is not my primary objective. I would prefer another team trophy because without a team we are nothing.

The closer the date came for the voting the more I was hoping to make it to the podium. Third place was the only position I could envisage, and I knew it would be between Luis Suarez, Gareth Bale, Neymar and me. I honestly never hoped to do better than that. Deep down you know it's the best you can do. In this game Ronaldo and Messi have been unbeatable. They are two monsters whose exploits will be talked about for years on end. Even my daughter and her children will hear about them. And why not also those of her dad!

I invited myself onto the table of the greats, so to speak, and, and it's now up to me to make sure I stay there. I want to continue dining with them! Ronaldo deserved his award. He won the Champions League and the Euros – in both cases against me – and he scored 51 goals and made 17 assists in 55 games. Every season, despite all the pressure, both he and Messi reach the top of their game.

Ronaldo was my neighbour, living in the La Finca area. At one time our houses were even next to each other and he would go past mine every day. We would exchange greetings, nothing more. I have since moved house but in the same residential complex. I met him by chance on holiday last year, just after the Euros. I was in Miami with Erika.

One evening we went to see a latino show. I was already in my seat when, totally by chance, Cristiano appeared with his friends.

After the show the place became a restaurant-discotheque. I went to find him and, laughing, I told him: "I hate you!" Then naturally I congratulated him on what he had achieved. I also told him that next year I hope it will be him congratulating me!

I admit I have a profound respect for him, just as I do for Messi. But we are different. Sometimes they appear as if they are in their bubble, completely ignoring the outside world, as if they are tired of being eternal objects of curiosity. For my part I'm quite chilled.

During a match at the Santiago Bernabeu, Real Madrid won a free-kick near the penalty area. Our wall began to get into position and Ronaldo placed the ball down. I went up to him to ask him where he was going to shoot. "I don't know," he replied.

"In the stand or in the net?" I said, winding him up. He didn't react. He took his run-up and the keeper pushed out his shot. I like having a bit of banter with an opponent, without provoking him or getting aggressive. These are attitudes I disapprove of. It's okay to do a bit of ribbing but not to humiliate.

At our place, in another game against Real, their Brazilian defender Marcelo was marking me. When we got a free-kick I sent a warning to him, laughing: "Watch out, I'm going to score." I knew that if I managed to get ahead of him when the ball came in I would score. But unfortunately I stayed blocked behind him and he cleared the ball. I need such moments of release.

For me, smiling and joking is essential.

(1) Antoine Griezmann succeeds Blaise Matuidi as the winner of the 2016 award. The voters are made up of former winners and the Editor of France Football
(2) Raymond Kopa died on March 3rd, 2017.

(3) A hot, South American herbal infusion.
(4) "See you tomorrow, my friends."
(5) Griezmann was voted third in the Ballon d'Or in both 2016 and 2018.
(6) The others are Raymond Kopa, Michel Platini, Jean-Pierre Papin, Zinedine Zidane, Just Fontaine, Alain Giresse, Jean Tigana, Eric Cantona, Thierry Henry and Franck Ribéry.
(7) He received his trophy at the Stade de France, just before the 2018 World Cup qualifier against Bulgaria.
(8) France's Professional Footballers' Association.

2

NEVER WITHOUT MY BALL

President, astronaut, pilot, doctor, engineer, lawyer, vet, scientist or actor: these are generally the jobs people say they want to do when they grow up. Me, I never wavered from my dream of becoming a professional footballer. That was all I thought about. Even when I was in primary school I was obsessed with being able to fulfil what was my passion. I wrote in my essays that I would later become a footballer. As far as I was concerned it was not open to debate. And I didn't have a plan B.

School wasn't exactly my thing. My favourite subject? Sport. I was terrible at maths, and I wasn't interested in history and geography. I didn't make any special effort. I sat right at the back of the class, next to the window. I'd often look out of it and see what was going on, working out how long was left before I could go and play football at break time. I wasn't very focused. I don't even know how I managed to pass my brevet des collèges. *(1)* Neither did my family. They've teased me often enough by asking how much I'd paid to get it! To be honest, I was lucky to have teachers who liked me and who weren't too strict.

The little blond kid that I was always had his football with him. Did I sleep with it? I can't remember. But I firmly believe that the people in the Les Gautriats neighbourhood never saw me without it! I would bring it with me even when I went to the local swimming pool.

Once, when I was going to school, my mum got hold of me and asked: "Antoine, are you sure you haven't forgotten something?"

"No, mum. I've got my ball," I replied, very sure of myself. However, I had left my school bag behind, which was obviously much less of a problem for me. The ball was never far from my rucksack. It helped me forget all my worries. It brought me happiness. It was my best friend.

At lunchtime, before or after eating, we used to organise mini tournaments. At the stadium, when I wasn't using the wooden goalposts, I used to train by aiming high at the triangular-shaped panels behind the basketball hoop, which became my goal.

Football, nothing but football. I used to bring my own ball there with my pals. I'm talking about a real one – the kind the professionals played with, made out of leather – even though it cost money. The other sports didn't matter to me. Today I am aware of the joy of being able to live my passion, especially as I was not very good at school. But, naturally, I know that education is important.

From as far back as I can remember, football has always been in my blood. I should acknowledge that there is a reason for this. My grandfather on my mother's side, Amaro Lopez, was a professional footballer. He was a defender. Not very big, but very tough, and I resemble him physically. He used to wear the yellow shirt of a club from Paços de Ferreira, a town in the north of Portugal, which lies between Porto and Guimarães. His team was called FC Vasco de Gama. In 1960 it changed its name to that of Football Club Paços de Ferreira, and it still operates today in the Portuguese first division, the Liga Sagres.

By the time the club had adopted this name my grandfather had left Portugal. Life was too difficult for him there and (António de Oliveira) Salazar's dictatorship, even though it was on the wane, was suffocating the country. He was married to Carolina and already had three children: José, Manuel and Maria Alriza.

France happened to be in need of manpower after the ravages of the Second World War, especially in the building trade. Amaro was a builder, and in 1956 he made the decision to get away. He did this all on his own because it was not an easy thing to do. As was the case with a lot of farmers he was unable to get hold of a tourist passport or emigration documents, so he went through clandestine channels. The way these structured networks were organised enabled him and a few brave men to enter France via an irregular crossing through Spain followed by a passage through the Pyrénées. The demands, both physical and financial, were significant.

Amaro first landed in Cassis, near Marseille, in the Bouches-du-Rhône, but he didn't like it there. The following year a certain Monsieur Couturier, who was a building contractor, approached him because he needed help in his business. That is how, in 1957, my grandfather settled in Mâcon, in the Saône-et-Loire region. Very quickly he brought over his wife and children. Amaro and Carolina's offspring would increase with the birth of Andrea and then Isabelle, my mum.

The Lopezes became the first Portuguese people to move to this town of just over 30,000 inhabitants, which is situated 65 kilometres north of Lyon. More generally, from the 1960s onwards, there was quite a large wave of Portuguese immigrants in France. In a decade they became the biggest foreign community in the country.

My grandmother made their integration easier, mainly by helping them with their administration formalities. Knocking on her door was an obvious thing to do. The most amazing thing was that she stood by them as they filled out their papers even though she was illiterate! Being unable to read or write never halted her enthusiasm nor her will to help. As for Amaro, he managed to carry on his activity as a builder until he became an invalid as a result of a serious accident. I don't have any memories of him, which is not too surprising considering he died in 1992, a year after I was born.

André Moreira is a Portuguese goalkeeper at Atlético Madrid. He is currently on loan at Aston Villa for the 2018/2019 season. He has spoken to me about my grandfather, explaining that he has seen photos of him in certain albums, notably in the book commemorating the 50th anniversary of the Paços de Ferreira club. The memory of Amaro Lopez also lives on through the indoor tournament that bears his name. It takes place once a year in the Mâcon Exhibition Centre each February. It is organised by the town's Sporting Club, which brings the Portuguese community together. My brother Théo plays for this club as a number nine.

My grandmother Carolina lived until 2009. It wasn't uncommon for her to look after us at her home. Towards the end of her life it was her turn to stay in our house. I was already at Real Sociedad. When I was younger I spent a few summer holidays in Portugal. I still have family in Paços de Ferreira, but I don't have any particular attachments there. My mum never spoke to us in her native tongue. She only did that with her own mother. One day I will find the time to go there and visit the Lopezes. What do I have about me that's Portuguese? It's got to be my grandmother's backside!

My dad, Alain, is a pure product of Mâcon. He never really knew the origins of his family name. His roots were in Alsace or Austria, where this name, literally, means 'wheat man' or 'gravel man'. However, his father, Victor, who was born in Orléans, resisted all things Mâcon.

My dad began playing football diligently from the age of nine at ASPTT Mâcon. He could play as a defender or midfielder, putting himself about a bit. In other words he would use his elbows and shoulders in order to get respect from his opponents. When he was at the top of his game his standard was equivalent to that of a player in the CFA, the fourth tier. He mainly operated in the reserve league in Saint-Étienne.

A qualified locksmith, he was offered a municipal post, 10 kilometres or so from the house, at La Chapelle-de-Guinchay, after he had finished national service. In return for work and lodging he had to take out a licence at the football club. He ended up playing in the district league, five divisions lower than before, in this village of about 3,000 souls on the cusp of the départements of the Ain and Rhône.

I owe everything to football. It is so true that it was through this sport that my parents met each other. When my father was playing at ASPTT Mâcon, his best friend happened to be Manuel Lopes. Born in Portugal, my future uncle could have tried to carve out a career as a professional because he was good. Like me, he could run all day. But his mum objected. She didn't want him to leave home. So when it came to choosing between football and family he didn't hesitate: he chose family. Even today he makes fun of my dad, saying that he was better than him and that I inherited his talent. My dad comes out with: "You had the skill, I had the intelligence. And in football it's intelligence which matters!"

Manuel was an attack-minded playmaker. He and my dad were club sponsors, from the same generation, and these two friends would continue to see each other even when my dad moved to La Chapelle-de-Guinchay.

To relax, they would go to a place on the quays, near Mâcon's town hall, where Isabelle, Manuel's sister, was one of the waitresses. She had started working there when she was 16 so she could help support her mum, who had five mouths to feed. She first trained at Les Tuileries brasserie and then, when she was older and allowed to serve alcohol, in a nearby bar which had the same owner. It was called *Le Paris* and later *Le Voltaire*.

My dad spotted this pretty girl, even though she looked a bit young – she is nine years younger than him. My uncle, who had become a carpenter, took on the role of match-maker. He himself was married and he encouraged their relationship to develop. The two lovebirds began dating and they soon made everything official. That's how, at 30 years of age, my dad married his team-mate's sister!

Maud was the product of this union on April 7th, 1988. My first cry came later, on March 21st, 1991, five years before Théo, who was born on August 30th, 1996 at the general hospital in Mâcon, where my mum used to work. Like Maud, I came into the world at the old maternity hospital in rue Chailly-Guéret, in Mâcon, which is now the only specialised unit for palliative care in the Saone-et-Loire.

Again, like Maud, I don't have a middle name. Théo has on his passport the names Victor and Amaro, which are those of his two grandfathers, who had recently passed away. For their first child my parents were quite happy to wait until the day to discover whether they were having a boy or a girl. Everyone had been convinced that it would be a boy and they had already chosen Antoine for the first name, especially my mum. Maud just held things up a little bit!

From the moment his daughter was born my dad significantly reduced his football commitments. Instead of going to play on a Sunday morning he would go for a walk and pick flowers with my mum, who didn't really like living in La Chapelle-de-Guinchay. So he asked to be transferred to Mâcon and he got his wish a few months after I was born. As a town employee he was given a staff house in the working-class neighbourhood of Les Gautriats, surrounded by trees and high-rise council flats. It was a former mansion which had been bequeathed to the municipality and converted into meeting rooms. My dad would wake up at 6.30am and then he'd come back and eat with us before returning to work, which consisted of maintaining and cleaning the buildings and sorting out any mechanical or electrical problems.

As a caretaker he would set his alarm every night at 11pm. He was also in charge of the nearby stadium with its multi-sport surface, which, apart from football, meant volleyball, handball or basketball could also be played there. At first there was no tarmac laid, so we used to play on sand. I kept asking for some goals and it was my dad who put them in. It goes without saying that very quickly I spent hours and hours there.

I loved this house and this environment, which was very quiet at the foot of the blocks of flats where I never ventured. I remember scratching the garage door – it was blue just like the shutters – when I was practising my shooting. Those marks will last forever. My parents lived in that house until 2013.

I was weaned on football. My dad was a volunteer coach for several teams and from all ages, from Under-9s to veterans. He coached the club of Thoissey, a little village in the Ain, for five years. It was a half hour journey there and I followed him almost every day. I watched every aspect closely but most of all I made the most of it by playing. I always brought my little football with me, exploiting every break in the sessions by going onto the pitch to juggle, dribble or shoot, either on my own or with friends. It didn't matter how late my father came home, and even with school the next morning, I was there. It was the same story at weekends when I went to the games with him.

My mum stopped working some years ago. I asked her to. In fact, she was suffering so much from burn-out that she was experiencing physical and nervous problems as a result of working hours on end and coping with all the stress. I understand that burn-out is the professional illness of the century. My mum put her heart and soul into everything. I watched her health suffer and that put me in a terrible state. She was exhausted.

In her first job as a waitress, she moved up through the ranks until her bosses entrusted her with the bar. She quit this job after Maud was born, my dad refusing to let her work until late at night. She continued to do housework for grannies and other people. Even the year she had off after my birth was busy because she helped her brother out, who had just bought a bar – of course. Then she found work at Onet Services, the cleaning company. She was posted to the general hospital in Mâcon, where she had to get up for work at 3.30am. But she would return at 11.15am to prepare our lunch. There again she had lots to do. She cleaned the rooms and the operating theatre before taking up a position of responsibility by being in charge of 40 people and signing contracts with Onet customers. She spent virtually every day of the year at that hospital.

Whenever she took on a project, she gave it everything she had. If a temp in her team called in sick, sometimes untruthfully, she would sacrifice herself and take their place. She compensated for absences, making every effort to find ways of filling in for people. She loved her work, but she had forgotten about its appeal. Her job was becoming too much for her and she was always tired. She felt ill and she no longer seemed to appreciate the times she came to see me. That couldn't go on. So I asked her to stop. I gave her no choice.

Of course, thanks to my wages at Atlético Madrid and my various contracts she didn't need to do any work at all. But she felt the urge, fearing that she would just go around in circles otherwise and get bored. I don't regret forcing her to take early retirement even though at the age of 51 she hasn't ruled out the idea of opening a bar/restaurant in Mâcon. That's an obsession.

My parents watched over us with love and tenderness. When we went shopping at Carrefour or Auchan they always used to buy us a little present. Now it's my turn to do whatever it takes to make them happy.

(1) National diploma awarded to pupils at the end of the equivalent of year 10.

3

IN THE FOOTSTEPS OF GIANTS

When I wasn't playing football, I was watching it. I was seven when France became World Champions, when their captain, Didier Deschamps, who is currently my national team coach, lifted the trophy in the Saint-Denis air on June 12th, 1998 after sweeping aside Brazil. I watched the match at home with the blue, white and red flag draped on the balcony. I watched that final wearing the France shirt. We cheered every goal. *And one, and two, and three zero!* After the victory we went out to the banks of the Saône, partying with our car horns.

During the preparations for the World Cup the France team had broken off to stop at the TGV railway station at Mâcon-Loché. Aimé Jacquet's men had had a training session at Saint-Jean-d'Ardières, to the north of Lyon. They were staying at the château of Pizay, a famous stronghold right in the middle of the Beaujolais vineyards which, during Euro

2016, welcomed the Northern Ireland delegation. The training session I was able to attend was held at the Arnas sports complex. We were taken there by the father of Jean-Baptiste Michaud, my best friend. JB had managed to go under the fencing to get Zidane to sign his football. Not me. I'd got other autographs but not Zizou's, much to my great disappointment. I was so shy that I never dared to ask. In its local news programme, the television channel M6 had shown a piece about Les Bleus being in the area and you could see two blond lads running after the players. Jean-Baptiste recently sent me the short footage.

With my dad, I had the chance to take in a lot of games. On a long car drive we even went once to Marseille to see Olympique de Marseille (OM), a team he liked. Jean-Baptiste came with us. It was the semi-final of the UEFA Cup in 1999 and I was eight years old. The Vélodrome was full, with Laurent Blanc, Peter Luccin, Daniel Bravo, William Gallas, Christophe Dugarry and Fabrizio Ravanelli on the pitch. There was no winner that night, nor were there any goals. In truth, I didn't really watch the game. The real spectacle was in the stands. I was fascinated by the Marseille fans, who sang throughout the match.

But the stadium I've been to the most is the Stade Gerland in Lyon. My father didn't have a season ticket but we used to go there often. First of all it was a matter of proximity because it's only an hour's drive from Mâcon. I had the pleasure of witnessing the start of Olympique Lyonnais' (OL) reign as French champions for seven consecutive years up to 2008.

I was there when the club won the first championship in its history, on May 4th, 2002, when they beat Lens, who were ahead of them in the table going into the final game. Generally

I used to go along the side of the pitch in the Jean-Jaurès stand and then I would go in the corner of the ground. That evening, full of joy, the midfielder Éric Carrière stood up and towered over the fencing in front of the moat. He was rejoicing, he wanted to share the moment with the fans, while some of them had already invaded the pitch. In the midst of all the euphoria Carrière had tossed away his shirt and his shorts and was only wearing his jockstrap! I wasn't far away from him, no doubt shouting my joy, but I was a bit stunned by it all.

The best atmosphere I've experienced as a supporter had come a bit earlier in December 2000. I had really wanted to soak up the derby fever between Lyon and their neighbours Saint-Étienne, so I got in with the Bad Gones, the most fanatical group of Lyon fans. I had never seen anything like it. I thought I was with a band of madmen. They screamed, they shouted, they were always moving. It was unbelievable. I got shoved around so much that I shifted myself onto a stair rail. But the whole thing was magical: Christophe Delmotte, with a fierce header, won the points – and a lot more – for OL against Les Verts in stoppage time.

In order to avoid the crowd and beat some of the traffic, a lot of fans left the Stade Gerland a few minutes before the final whistle, but we stayed right to the end. As soon as the players made their way to the dressing room we ran back to the car so as not to get caught up in traffic jams as best we could. Often my mum would come with us and I had to wolf down a kebab before the game.

In December and January, the cold caught up with us. I remember an OL-OM game during this period which I attended with my cousin, Dominique Martins, where we were so frozen that we put plastic bags on our feet. Pitou, which is what everyone called him, had even given me his socks so I could keep warm! Lyon had a fantastic team. I don't claim to have a titanic football knowledge or an infallible memory, but I can remember the rabonas produced by the Brazilian defender Edmilson, who was a 2002 World Cup winner, whose passes just flew to the forward players. I also remember the drag back by Fred, his compatriot, in the Champions League against PSV Eindhoven, which he followed by pushing the ball past a defender, running onto it the opposite side, and lashing a shot into the roof of the net.

My two favourite players in this OL team were also Brazilians. How I loved Sonny Anderson, who had arrived from Barcelona in 1999, and also Juninho, who wore the number eight shirt. His free-kicks from distance were a work of art, with their quite astonishing trajectory. Especially those he scored against Real Madrid or Barcelona when the yellow-shirted captain was virtually in the corner. I also remember the ones he got against Ajaccio from almost in the middle of the park, 40 metres from goal, or against Werder Bremen when the ball floated first to the right, then to the left and then to the right again before hitting the net. As soon as he got close to striking the ball the fans would chant his name: Juninho! I almost know all his goals by heart.

My role models were everywhere. From a hairstyle point of view I used to resemble Pavel Nedved, the Juventus and Czech Republic playmaker. I was dark blond and I asked my mum to change my hair colour so I could have the same long light blond look as the former Ballon d'Or winner.

While David Beckham remains my idol for his class on and off the field, I was also a fan of Didier Drogba. When he was at OM he used to wear blue studs, whereas mine were silver.

So one afternoon at home I coloured my studs blue before I went training.

I also collected autographs of Lyon players. My dad knew one of the people in charge of the medical staff of the club, Patrick Perret, who, by the way, is still its physio/osteopath. We used to meet him at the Château de Pizay, where OL went the night before games and where I could get hold of the players. I was very reserved and so it was my dad who took photos after he had checked it was okay. I posed with Pierre Laigle, Vikash Dhorasoo, Philippe Violeau, Tony Vairelles and Sonny Anderson, my favourite of all, whose shirt I managed to get hold of. However, the long-sleeved one with Karim Benzema's name on, I had to buy.

There's another aspect of the whole football theatre which is of great importance to me: goal celebrations. When I used to score I would slide as far as possible on my knees, as I had seen Fernando Torres do. I used to run towards the corner flag and then it began. I started this with my friends when I was very small. When we went to watch the veterans in Mâcon we used to play together before each game and also at half-time. It was the opportunity to look for my signature celebration, one which I hope kids will remember and be keen to reproduce.

During Euro 2016 I celebrated my second goal against Ireland with a nod to the Canadian rapper Drake, waving both my hands with my thumbs and little fingers extended as if I was holding two telephones. It was a reference to how he appears in his 'Hotline Bling' video. I carried this on in the Euros and the thing seemed to work well because a lot of people copied it. Some went as far as replacing Drake's face with mine in a parody of the video. I liked this so much that I posted it on my Twitter and Facebook pages.

When I was little, I enjoyed trying to stop goals almost as much as scoring them. The ritual began with putting on the gloves. I quite liked that soft sensation. And then diving, what pleasure I got, whether it was on grass or on hard floors during indoor tournaments. My dad sent me on a two-week course to Hauteville, in the Ain region. On the agenda was football in the morning and various activities in the afternoon. When I got home I handed him the tape which the organisers had given to us so that parents could see how we had got on.

When my dad saw that I was often in goal he became annoyed. "That's not right. I'm not paying for you to go on a course so you can end up in goal," he muttered. I still love diving around. Even today, at Atlético, at the end of training, I sometimes go in goal to knock away a few shots. I wait for the coach to disappear before I go sliding about. I am the only outfield player in the squad to do this. Even at home, when my friends are around, I enjoy going in goal in the garden.

Charnay-lès-Mâcon is the club where I got my first licence, in the poussin *(1)* age group. We used to play our games at the Stade de la Massonne. Jean-Baptiste Michaud, whom I asked to be godfather to my daughter, Mia, was also there. I have fond memories of Bruno Chetoux, who was one of the coaches there when I started out. Later on there were Christophe Grosjean and Jérôme Millet.

The club of Charnay then merged with Mâcon, and the Union du football mâconnais (UFM) was born. I played there with the Under-13s and who was my coach? My dad, of course! When we let in a goal it was always my fault! He was tougher on me, more demanding, as if to show that despite our family ties I was in no way benefiting from any favouritism. That gave me mental strength and I began to think about being a team player. He often used to yell at me but when he brought me home everything would be forgotten.

The serious stuff began on the field. We were the tournament terrors, winning quite a lot of local competitions and we were champions of Bourgogne (Burgundy). I wasn't great in defeat and I could cry with rage. Several of us were frail looking and on the small side, like Jean-Baptiste, our central defender, or me. And yet we were the giant-slayers. I adored my dad's training sessions. He made you into a man before he made you into a footballer, and everyone had their chance. I was generally playing on the wing or as a centre-forward and my left foot would be the difference in games. My dad coached the UFM Under-19s for a long time and after a two-and-a-half year break he looked after the Under-13s whom he took three times a week. He loves passing on his knowledge. He used to miss that adrenalin buzz.

Another coach I had was Jean Belver, who was in charge of the team with Thierry Comas, a former fourth division player with Louhans-Cuiseaux. Belver used to supervise the 14-year-olds and because I was in a higher age group he looked after me. He was a real character. His sessions contrasted sharply with what I had already come across. It was almost a revolution, full of intensity and laughter, too. He made us work on our heading and our jumping. Also, so we could gain strength as well as power he made us strike the ball with our bare feet. That was novel.

At first I wondered where he was going with this lunacy. But he was right. This apprenticeship took place at the end of training: without anyone in the goal he used to ask us to hit the ball as hard as possible so that it would cross the line without touching the ground. My feet toughened up, and it wasn't that painful. Then he would teach us a different way of kicking the ball, allowing more variety in our shots.

I still find this exercise useful because my boots only weigh 100 grammes. They are thin and ultra-light. I like that sensation. It's as if I'm not wearing anything! I'm laying claim to this model, which is twice as light as the traditional football boot.

Jean Belver passed away aged 95, on October 27th, 2016. He represented France on one occasion and played for Stade de Reims, Lyon and Marseille. He was also captain of OGC Nice, notably in 1952, the year when they won the French League and Cup double. Because of his ability to develop young talent, this leader of men earned the nickname 'the wizard'.

I have never forgotten him.

(1) Eight to 10 year-olds.

4

UPROOTED

The smell of childhood and its intoxicating aromas of nostalgia and emotion ... I need to go back to my roots on a regular basis.

My particular mark on Mâcon is being left with the Antoine Griezmann Challenge, which has taken place each June on four synthetic pitches in the Stade Nord in since 2013. It is organised by the *Team Grizi* association, which I put in place. It's a way of giving back to the town that gave so much to me and an opportunity to see the smiles on the children's faces. I try to attend so I can sign autographs, pose for photos and present the awards. Hundreds of kids have competed against each other at Under-9s, Under-11s and Under-13s level. Volunteers take care of the 60 teams and the proceeds have been donated to the municipal associations.

Team Grizi is a family affair. The association is presided over by my dad, and my mum is the vice-president. I am proud of this Challenge, which serves as a homage to all the tournaments in which I have taken part. I leave it to my dad to organise everything. The only things I ask are these: that a big cup is given to the winning team, and that the best player, top scorer and best keeper are singled out. In the final we play the Champions League music when the teams take to the field. My parents see to everything, taking care of the slightest detail, such as looking after the snack bar, the merguez sausages, the vin d'honneur *(1)* and so on.

Mâcon is home. As soon as I have two days off I go there to rest. It's just a natural thing to do. I don't need to go out. I just stay indoors, in the family cocoon. It's the ideal place to cut yourself off from things. I don't move, I listen to conversations, I chill. I sniff the steam of the food which my mum is preparing as it filters from the kitchen, I hear my dad moan and my brother come home from school. It's just routine! Besides, even today when, with Maud, who lives in Paris, we speak of home it's only ever about Mâcon. I never had my own room. I shared with my sister, whose room was right next to my parents'. There were no posters of footballers on the walls. Instead I used to sleep under a duvet whose colours were in the colours of Olympique Lyonnais. Maud was alone in that room after I left for the Basque country, but goodness knows my exile was slow in taking shape! It got me down.

My useful performances in Mâcon had increased my reputation in the region and beyond. Clubs began to watch me, scouts asked me to come for trials. My dad used to go with me. I wouldn't say he was pushing me into it but he wasn't dissuading me either, such was my desire to make it as a footballer. I had to go for it.

Jean-Baptiste, who was generally a playmaker, was doing the same thing. He went on to join the academy at Gueugnon, in the Sâone-et-Loire, but that quickly came to an end. After living in Mexico he returned to Mâcon, where he is now a supervisor in a middle-school. But we rubbed shoulders during the trials.

My first one took place in Auxerre. I was supposed to stay there for a couple of weeks but I ended up staying a month. I thought I'd be sleeping at their academy set-up but I was lodged in a youth hostel.

At the time Djibril Cissé and Philippe Mexès were starring in the first team. I loved Mexès, a blond and elegant defender. I had the chance to watch the pros train a few times. Auxerre believed I had talent, but I wasn't kept on.

Lyon was next on the list. Three other young players of my age saw their qualities develop: Alexandre Lacazette, Clément Grenier and Yannis Tafer. Especially Alex, who was already banging the goals in. The murmur about him was flattering. "Look, it's Lacazette," people used to say. He deserved that recognition. We became pals in France's Under-18s before we won the Euro Under-19s together. One way of measuring how far I've come is by me asking him: "Do you remember when Lyon didn't take me on?"

For a year, my father took me every Wednesday to train for an hour at OL, at the Plaine des Jeux de Gerland. In reality Lyon had thought about offering me a so-called non-solicitation agreement (ANS) which would have been registered by the League's legal board. In other words while I was playing in Mâcon's 14-year-olds age group, the club had two years to offer me a contract. If this didn't happen then OL would pay me compensation. For my part, I wasn't allowed to sign for anyone else for three years. Of the five people at OL who made the decision about the ANS, two weren't in favour of signing me. They believed there were better footballers around.

When they closed the door on me, they came out with something like: "Your son is good, but we are going to take a bit more time. We'll leave him at his club in Mâcon so he can continue his development. We'll keep an eye on his progress..." I have heard this speech many times. Sometimes I'd get discouraged and I wouldn't feel like going to trials. My father insisted: "Hang on in there. If it works out you'll love it. It will be a dream for you."

It was then the turn of Sochaux and Saint-Étienne to say no. I was approaching 14. The journey back home with my dad seemed so long and the disillusionment was still burning inside. I wasn't in the best of moods. I even had to have X-rays on my wrist, so they could see if I was growing correctly and how tall I might become! It was painful. Clubs were mostly looking for big players, powerful and physical, without changing their profiles too much. They neglected to think about the future. The selection criteria consisted of testing your speed over 40 metres. If you didn't run it in a minimum time you were eliminated. It was an odd view of what makes a footballer.

The next trial took me to Metz. On this occasion my dad and I were accompanied by Geoffrey, my godfather. After a long day on the road, they slept in a hotel while I was put up at the academy. All the beds bore the crest of FC Metz. I was fascinated by the décor and by the atmosphere. I could see myself there already. I played a half in a friendly against Stuttgart and then the match after that.

This time things seemed to be going well. The proof being that the person in charge asked us to come back the following week for another trial. "Your son has talent," he told my dad. "We want to see him again. We'll pay your expenses." So we went back to the Moselle *(2)*. Once again I felt good. The things

I was told were positive: "In principle it's good. I'll confirm everything to you in the week, but we should be taking your son. You'll be able to see him as often as you want. He will be with us during the week and he'll go back home by train at weekends to play for Mâcon. We'll pay for the journey." In my mind it was all done and dusted. I was mentally prepared.

A week on and there was no news. Then three more weeks... and still no confirmation. As it turned out, the head of the academy wouldn't call. It was through a Metz scout that we finally learned that I wasn't selected and there was no real explanation for it. It was horrible. It was one big slap in the face. When I found out I locked myself in my room for several hours, crying with anger. I couldn't stand it. I wanted to stop with the football.

Metz clearly has problems when it comes to unearthing talent: Michel Platini, when he was a cadet *(3)* in Jœuf, had been failed on a pre-selection course at FC Metz after the doctor there had judged his breathing capacity to be insufficient, following a spirometer *(4)* test!

I was wounded, permanently so, by Metz not letting me through their door. Lens then contacted my dad, who turned down their offer of a trial for me. He was resigned to what would happen and he wanted to spare me another disappointment. But I am not a vindictive person. I prefer to look at the positives. Being taken on by Metz would not have guaranteed I turned professional. Ironically, it's thanks to these failures that I am where I am. The "no, sorry, he is too small," doubtless galvanised me. That was my good fortune! The little blond kid with the long hair and the two earrings found the motivation needed to make the breakthrough.

When someone is 13 I believe the most important thing

is not to know if a player is capable of running 100 metres in ten seconds and will grow to 6'5" tall when he's an adult, but to detect if he is talented enough to play at the highest level. At the time the academies were looking for immediate results. They went for the easy option rather than focusing on a player's development. And as I was very thin when I was younger the big strapping galoots would get in ahead of me. It was infuriating because I was scoring lots of goals when I wasn't even playing as a centre-forward.

Fortunately, fate intervened during a new trial, this time with Montpellier. On the first weekend of May 2005, a club scout invited me to play for them in an international and regional tournament for 13-year-olds. It was created by Paris Saint-Germain (PSG) and called the Bernard Brochand Challenge, named after a former club official, who was also deputy mayor of Cannes. The competition was held in Saint-Germain-en-Laye, at the Camp des Loges, where PSG usually trained. My dad took me to Montpellier with another friend, Steve Antunes, who was also having a trial. From there we made the trip to the capital in the TGV *(5)*. Unlike the other kids, I didn't go there wearing the Montpellier jersey but a Jamaica shirt.

As I was getting out of the van which dropped us off on pitch side, a gentleman I didn't know smiled at me. "I didn't know Jamaica were coming?!" That was my first contact with Éric Olhats. I didn't pay much attention, I just played my game and took a break.

I had some Petit Écolier *(6)* biscuits in my bag. I ate them as I sat in the stands watching the game. Then the man came up to me again. "I'll swap you a pin badge of your team for a biscuit," he says. Quick as a flash I reply: "I don't want your pin badge. But, here, I'll give you a Petit Écolier!" And that's how our association began.

Based in Bayonne, Éric had come to look at some of the future talents and to assess whether they were able to train with Real Sociedad in Spain. I didn't exactly shine in this mini-tournament. I scored a goal against a rather weak team, with a long distance shot. At the end of the day, while I was drinking a Sprite on the pitch and waiting for the award presentations, I noticed Éric near the bench. He came over to me and asked if he could have a drink. I offered him my bottle and he handed me his business card, which he took from the pocket of his shorts. He had written a little message on it. "Here, read this when you get home to Mâcon," he suggested before slipping away.

He may have asked me not to read it before I got home, but the temptation was too great and, obviously, I couldn't resist. I read what he had written on his business card on the journey back. He introduced himself as a scout, adding this bit for my parents: *I would like your son to have a week's trial at Real Sociedad. Call me.*

My parents weren't home. They had treated themselves to a fortnight's holiday in Croatia. I let them know about my news. My dad was sceptical. He was convinced it was some sort of bad joke which one of his friends had come up with. But I kept at him.

When he got back, because I wasn't letting the matter drop, he called Éric, raising his voice to dispel the possibility of it all being a hoax. "Right, who is this? Cut all this crap. Tell me who you are. I've got better things to do..."

Very quickly he began to see that Éric Olhats wasn't kidding. I really wanted a crack at this. Just like the other clubs, there had been no follow-up from Montpellier. It was the usual blah-blah-blah: "We're sorry we can't take your son on, but we will keep track of his progress..."

Despite speaking to Éric, my dad still feared that Real Sociedad was a complete waste of time, while my mum thought it was too far away. What's more, the trial was due to last for a week, which is longer than any I had experienced up till then. But I was motivated. It was scheduled for the summer holidays and it gets hot in Spain.

Having got the okay from my parents, I immediately spent a week at Éric's apartment in Bayonne, ten minutes away from the Atlantic Ocean. It's difficult to forget my first match: I arrived just in time for the final of a small tournament against the neighbours and rivals Athletic Bilbao. I had barely been on the pitch when I scored the winning goal with a header from a corner. It goes without saying that things started off with a bang. The other players were a year older than me. I was especially struck by the fact that there were other small players there, some even smaller than me! Spain had understood that it's not just size which matters. The players took time to speak to me, to encourage me and to come out with the odd word in French. They gave me the ball so that I could show what I could do, whereas in France it was generally every man for himself. Here everyone played together. The team came first. Needless to say that came as quite a change.

It turned out to be a rewarding week, one of satisfaction. In order to rubber-stamp my trial, Real Sociedad, who are based in San Sebastián, wanted me for a second week. It was so they could see me train with people of my own age-group, who were returning from a tournament. Once again, everything happened simply. I didn't speak a word of Spanish, but then football is a universal language. And whenever I didn't understand the instructions, Éric wasn't far away to translate for me. I had the feeling of being on a dream break, as if I had gone on a two-week holiday.

I returned to Mâcon with a sense of achievement. But I didn't want to get carried away. I was afraid of being disappointed. This time, however, I felt good. In the meantime I had resumed my daily life, going between school and training at the Union du football mâconnais. I was playing with my cousin Pitou in the stadium at the foot of our house when I saw Éric turn up. He had driven all the way from Bayonne. The atmosphere was relaxed as he joined in with us on the artificial pitch.

Then, in the late afternoon, he came to the house to talk to my parents. He was the bearer of some excellent news: Real Sociedad's sporting director had agreed I could join the club. I was so happy. I couldn't take in what was happening. I could see myself there already. La Liga was mine... My parents, though, weren't as enthusiastic. Bayonne was an eight-hour car journey away and my mum, particularly, wasn't convinced.

"I want to go, let me leave," I insisted. In the end they gave in. But by agreeing my dad warned Éric: "I'm leaving him with you. Make sure he doesn't get up to any nonsense."

I left Mâcon in August at the age of 13 for the Basque region, in the far south-west of the country. It was the start of a new existence with classes at the Saint–Bernard de Bayonne middle-school and training with Real. I didn't care that I was saying goodbye to mum's delicious cooking!

The very first time I travelled with Éric was on May 25th, 2005. I remember the day because, after a good journey, we slept in a small hotel to recover from the tiredness. The

Champions League final between AC Milan and Liverpool in Istanbul was on television. It was a memorable match, which had an improbable comeback and an incredible scenario: Liverpool were getting beaten 3-0 at half-time and within seven minutes they had drawn level. Xabi Alonso, who played for Real Sociedad the previous season, got the final goal in normal time, scoring from the rebound after his penalty was saved. Backed by their wonderful fans, who were there in force, Steven Gerrard's Reds won in the penalty shoot-out. While we were watching the game I assured Éric: "Don't worry. We're going to play for this Cup and we're going to win it!"

I had never been far away from my family. So in order that I wasn't totally lost Éric wanted me to stay at his place. I was relieved about this. He knew that if I was boarding or living with a family I would probably have cracked and that I would have been tempted to go back home earlier than expected.

My classes ran from 8am to midday. I would then go to the canteen before returning to class until 4.30pm. The lessons were very strict and weren't always my thing. As was the case in Mâcon, I sat at the back and, I admit, I didn't hesitate to look over the shoulder of the person next to me so I could copy. My homework wasn't top notch – I often got home from training about 10pm – and I'd borrow one of my friend's pens because I'd forgotten my stuff. I was miles away. I was an average pupil. Sometimes I deliberately missed a lesson. I just preferred to play football and, so as to escape class, I used to hide in the toilets!

Tired of all this, the head-teacher finally told Éric that I was skipping class. In response he yelled at me, which he often did and rightly so. He wasn't just being strict. One day my Spanish teacher, who was also my form teacher, opened up to him about this: "What does Antoine want? He only thinks about football. He should get it into his head that he will never be a footballer. He should stop talking in class and stop dreaming. He's got to study." On the one hand she was right. I'm obviously aware of how important it is to have a good education. In football a lot of people try their luck and few actually make it. But what she said made an impression on me. I had been cut to the quick, and it made me even more motivated to succeed and to show her that she had been wrong about me.

As soon as the bell rang at the end of lessons I used to walk to the neighbouring tennis club, about 100 metres away, where I would wait for Éric. In his Volkswagen van he would collect the young French kids he'd looked after at middle-school and high school and take us the 50 or so kilometres to training at Real Sociedad, at the academy in the village of Zubieta. We used to go past the Anoeta Stadium, with its athletics track around the pitch, where the first team play.

"Look, this is where I'm going to play and score later on," I said to Éric, who thought it amusing. He was being careful, trying to temper my enthusiasm so that I wouldn't really believe it. "No, no, that's impossible." Even today I sometimes say to him: "Do you remember when we went past the stadium?" I was the smallest person in his seven or eight-seater van and I sat next to him in the front. Bonds of friendship were formed between us all and on the field I tried to adapt as quickly as possible. I was clinging on to my ambition of becoming a footballer, of one day playing in front of 50,000 fans.

I paid great attention to my surroundings. I didn't take private Spanish lessons but, through hearing the conversations in the dressing room, things began to sink in. I also listened to a lot of songs: it's an effective way of learning a language.

Whenever I had doubts about my footballing ability Éric cheered me up. "Don't go beating yourself up," he would encourage me. "Just play like you did for your club in Mâcon and everything will be fine." He told me over and over again that he believed in me and that I should keep at it. His message was: "I'm warning you: it won't be easy every day. Sometimes you'll feel very close to breaking point. But it's worth sticking in there. I know that when I take you to football everything will be all right. You'll forget all your worries. Trust me. I'll be there…" He was right.

Despite everything, having my family so far away wasn't easy. Leaving the people who are close to you at such a young age was like being torn apart. My parents were working and it wasn't practical for them to come over at weekends. I went home for school holidays but it was all too short. The journey from the house to Lyon Saint-Exupéry airport to go to Biarritz, 10 kilometres from Bayonne, was awfully long…

It was only my dad who took me to the airport. It was too painful for my mum. And for me. I cried in the back of the car. Every time, just before the Villefranche-sur-Saône toll that led us to the motorway, he would stop and turn towards me. "So, do we stop or what?" he'd ask. "If you want to come back home there's no problem…" He gave me the choice.

I had only signed for a licence at Real Sociedad, not a contract. Even though the expenses were paid I wasn't getting any money. I was a free man. But I had no intention of quitting. After a few seconds, as I dried my eyes with the back of my sleeve, I said to him: "No, dad. I want to make it." And we carried on towards Lyon Saint-Exupéry.

All the return trips to Bayonne proved difficult, and I mean all. How can you forget these tears? My mum couldn't escape them. On the days when she decided to come with us, her tears fell on her glasses. She would always look straight ahead, as if she had been forbidden to look behind her. But it was only to spare me her sadness. Nevertheless, she didn't know that I could see her sorrow in the mirror. My dad displayed no such emotion. He was focused to the extreme. I never saw him cry. But it must have been so painful knowing that his son was full of tears behind him, knowing as well that he wouldn't be able to hug him in his arms for several months.

Every time on the journey I would replay things that we had experienced as a family, the outings where we would put the world to rights, mum's meals, my dad coming home from work and the wait for my brother to return from school before we could eat. I missed birthdays, those small everyday things which are the essence of life. I have missed all those moments, and from time to time I still do! At the time my passion for football was so strong that I still managed to get onto the plane to Biarritz.

At first, relations with Éric may have been strained at times. We both had to find our feet, so to speak, our best way of dealing with things. He did the best he could. It was the first time he had allowed anyone to live at his place. It wasn't part of the original plan but it was best for everyone. The fact Éric is still with me and is still my sporting adviser whom I call each day, demonstrates the strong relationship which unites us. I have blind faith in him. I consider him to be my mentor and, instead of being an agent, he and my dad take care of my future.

Still, it wasn't always easy. Towards November, when the weather began to get colder and the days shorter, I would get a bit depressed every year. If Éric hadn't have taken me in I'd have gone back home on December 1st, especially as I didn't have too many friends at school.

When my parents called me to see how things were I'd tell them everything was fine. But they guessed that wasn't always the case. Parents can sense these sort of things. It's true that I sometimes wrote text messages when I was crying, in total darkness. There were brief moments when I even thought about giving it all up. It was hard to motivate myself, of course, but, as Éric used to say, once I was out on that field everything was forgotten. I trained hard. He would bring me back every evening and, very often, we would only get to the house in Bayonne at 10pm because he had to drop off the other kids he looked after. I was tired and too exhausted to do all my homework.

We also had to cook. Neither Éric nor I was very good at that. We'd do our shopping at the supermarket and we'd be happy enough to heat up a frozen ready meal in the microwave and eat it in front of the television before going to bed. The only things I knew how to do were to cook a steak haché *(7)* and heat up pasta and rice.

Sometimes, at weekends, for his work as a Real Sociedad scout, he would travel around France to take in games and spot young talent and I'd find myself alone. Suddenly I grew up and learned about being responsible, even though my agenda was simple in his absence: watch football on television and play on the PlayStation.

Éric's apartment was on the top floor of a block in the heart of Bayonne. It's a town which has character, a population of almost 50,000 and stands at the foot of the Pyrenees. Its gothic cathedral is a World Heritage Site. Its motto rings true with the Basques, if I may say so: *Nunquam polluta*, which means 'never defiled,' a reminder that it managed to resist 14 sieges. Éric lived 50 metres from the Albert Camus middle-school, which suited me fine because it was there where, from my second year onwards at Real, I had my classes. But football remained the priority. Having a club licence without a contract meant I began to earn a bit of money: about 6,000 euros a year.

When Éric drove us in his hired van I would occasionally doze off, especially when the sun was in my face. I'd close my eyes a little and Éric would take that opportunity to give me a little slap on the back of my head to wake me up. He didn't want me turning up at training asleep. He was demanding and a little army-like. When he was at the wheel he used to put on the music he liked, from Led Zeppelin to Chuck Berry. I shouldn't need to tell you that it wasn't exactly the kind of stuff I'd listen to. I preferred it when one of his pals brought us back: we had the choice of music.

This period of my life was character building. Today I am ready and prepared to face anything that happens. I lived in my bubble, which is why I still find it hard to talk about myself, to speak of my emotions. I'm not one who confides in people or who openly expresses his feelings ... until this book. I avoided complaining during my years as an apprentice. I gritted my teeth and, in the event of a problem, I wouldn't really let on to Éric or my parents, even though they weren't fooled.

There were hardly any arguments. I don't like conflict and, in general, I manage to avoid it. As it happens I didn't really experience adolescence. When I felt the need to clear my head I would go to the cinema. Of course, I did do some silly things for my age. Youth must have its fling, as the saying goes. Oh, there was nothing out of the ordinary. For example a friend and I borrowed Éric's van to go and collect our order from McDonald's because we couldn't be bothered to walk there. Except, of course, that neither of us had a driving licence. Naturally the van kangarooed a little. We confessed all this to him a few years later. I still had this obsession with *McDo* when I hopped on his lovely bike to go and get food. Again there were two of us, one on the seat and the other on the luggage rack. The bike broke on the way back. The chain had gone. Because we were unable to fix it we had to confess to everything. Éric was pretty miffed!

In Bayonne, I used to go out quite a lot with Théo Lator, and I'd often go round to his house. We'd get out and about, making the most of our freedom and our youth. When I went back to Mâcon for the holidays I'd go, as most people did, to Club 400, the town's disco, or to La Clé des Chants, half an hour away. This was a more spacious place, with four dance halls and as many different atmospheres. I went there a few times with my friends.

I didn't experience what you might call a classic youth. Because I was wrapped up in football I wasn't able to reply to party invitations from people in my class. I either had a match or I had training. In any case, Éric wouldn't let me go out. He didn't want me to drive his scooter, which he considered to be too dangerous or sleep over at Théo's. He demanded I came home every night. He was a bit Père Fouettard *(8)*, a bit child minder, a bit big brother, a bit shrink, a bit mate. Basically he was a bit of everything. He knew that football at the highest level required discipline and that success can quickly drift away. He was just as obstinate with girls. In the last year when I was sleeping at his place he wouldn't let me go out with a girlfriend.

He was strict, but at the same time we had some great laughs. We did loads of things together, such as go-karting or tenpin bowling. He took me to several games, where he had to write reports about future talents he had spotted with a view to bringing them to Real Sociedad. He took me to Bordeaux, where he went to watch some players. As usual, he was listening to his music on the way there. He could see I was angry and he said to me: "If you're not happy you can remove the CD." And that's what I did. I took it and I threw his Chuck Berry album out of the window!

After this episode, in Bordeaux with Éric, I discovered the inner world of professional football. He asked me in the stands to look at the game. "Then you will tell me who you liked and who you didn't. And we'll compare notes." I loved it. This was my world. I didn't miss a thing, paying close attention to every detail on and around the field. Éric tried to make me laugh every day when he felt I was slowing down or I needed cheering up. He took care of me. As far as he was concerned I had to concentrate on football and only football. And not to lose focus. Although this kind of approach frightened me a little, he was right. He would give me advice all the time. He attended some of my training sessions and all of my games, emphasising the things he had liked and pointing out my faults. His method was effective.

One day when he had brought me back from training we arrived home late, as was often the case. He mulled things over and, a few minutes later, he encouraged me to follow him. We got back into the car and, without any explanation, he decided to take me to the sea front, barely five minutes away.

He wasn't happy with how I'd done. He considered that my reaction time had been slow. So he took out the balls from

Father and son: Yes, it's really me. I'm four years old and I'm posing with my dad Alain, a footballer with ASPTT Mâcon and a volunteer coach

First steps: I have just learned how to walk and I'm thrilled to show everyone in front of my grandmother Carolina's house in Mâcon

Happy holidays: With my parents, Isabelle and Alain, my sister Maud and my little brother Théo in the buggy. We are on holiday in Séte, as we were every summer of my adolescence

Game time: At the Vias camp site in the Hérault. For once, I'm leaving the ball alone to show off at pétanque, a game which I'm really passionate about

Too small: Having a trial at Olympique Lyonnais (OL) in 2001 notably with my friend Stéphane, with whom I played at l'Union Football Mâconnais (UFM). Unfortunately, once again, I won't be kept on

Sonny day: I go very often to the Stade Gerland to see Lyon's games. My two favourite players are Brazilian: Juninho and the striker Sonny Anderson, whose nose for a goal is amazing. I'm posing here with him during one of OL's match preparations

Team shot: I'm 10 years old – at the bottom to the right – next to my UFM team-mates. We are the terrors of the region. Mâcon is the only French club I've played for!

Celebration time: In the kitchen in 2002, with my grandmother, my sister and my brother. I'm still wearing the OL shirt...

All together: The whole family, in 2014, outside our childhood home in Mâcon, where we would gather for Christmas each year. My wife Erika is in the second row, second from the right

Big break: In 2005, thanks to Éric Olhats, who spotted me, I sign for Real Sociedad in San Sebastián. I'm living at Éric's in Bayonne, but sometimes my family come to visit. Here my parents are with my cousins Magalie and Pitou

Hunting the ball: During a Real Sociedad training session in 2009, where I'm tracking my team-mate and friend Emilio Nsue

Acrobatics: My scissor-kick for Real Sociedad against OL at Gerland in the first leg play-off game for the Champions League in 2013. This enabled us to win (2-0) and me to get known in France!

Up against the best: Keeping up with Andrés Iniesta in a league match against Barcelona in 2013

Stepping up: So proud to pull on the France shirt. Didier Deschamps gave me my first call-up in 2014

Spice boy: Celebrating a goal for my new club Atlético Madrid. It had to be the number 7 shirt for me – like David Beckham

the boot and switched on the headlights because it was dark, and he directed the lights towards a low wall. Next he put several blocks on the ground. Then, with each shot, he asked me to move towards the wall and I had to control the ball or do a pass without the ball touching the ground. I repeated this exercise for some time. I was out of breath, but I hung on. This drill went on for so long that by the time we wanted to go back the car battery was flat because Éric had left his lights on! He had to call a friend just before midnight, who came to our rescue with some jump leads, which helped us get the engine going.

The night time session was helpful. My speed on the pitch and my ability to get forward quicker were partly perfected on the Bayonne waterfront.

(1) Reception.
(2) The département in Lorraine where Metz is situated.
(3) Age group for 13-14 year-olds.
(4) An apparatus for measuring the volume of air inspired and expired by the lungs.
(5) Train à Grande Vitesse, France's high-speed train.
(6) A brand of chocolate biscuit.
(7) Chopped beef which is made into a burger, minus the bun.
(8) A character who accompanies St. Nicholas in his rounds on December 6th dispensing lumps of coal and/or floggings to naughty children while St. Nicholas offers gifts to those who have been good. He is known mainly in the far north and eastern regions of France.

5

A PICTURE OF FAME

Sonny Anderson and other Lyon stars were the famous footballers I admired when I was growing up. Now young fans look up to me as a star player. The smile which appears on children's faces when I pose for a photo with them or sign an autograph is always a joy.

I don't know if any of the children who get their pictures taken with me will go on to be professionals but in any case I hope their parents will know how to encourage them within the realms of what is acceptable. It bothers me when I see dads and even mums moaning non-stop during a game in which their children are playing. I came across a video where parents were actually fighting each other during their son's match.

Too many adults fill their kids' heads with hopes which are unrealistic. Instead of pushing them towards being professionals, they would be better off teaching them how to enjoy just being on the field. That's all that matters.

My dad is a football coach and even though he supported me, he never forced things. He behaved the same way with my brother. He used to take me to training, but in December, when it was cold and Théo didn't fancy going he respected his choice. Otherwise my brother would have been demoralised by football.

In everything I accomplish, I strive to give a good image of my sport. Smiling is also a way of showing that some players, in this particular field, don't take themselves too seriously. That explains some of my popularity. Nothing is fabricated. I'm not playing any game. I know very well that some supporters and journalists have favourite players. I'm not going to change their opinion: anyway, I don't read what's written about me. I know whether or not I've played well.

For example, I have refused to do any kind of media training. I don't want to be shaped. I intend to keep my spontaneity and my freshness, even though I'm aware that my French is not always brilliant, since I speak Spanish every day. Occasionally I'll forget my words or not know how to say things, but I accept that. This is me. No way will I be a robot. I want people to like me for what I am, not for how others would want me to be. And if they don't happen to like me, then that's just too bad.

I am lucky to be liked. This is illustrated in several ways. One example a few years ago was being picked to go on the front cover of FIFA 16. A vote was taken on the Internet and I got the most votes, finding myself alongside Lionel Messi. That was a dream. When I started out as a professional, I would never have imagined such recognition. But it was on the French sleeve. One day I hope to appear on the worldwide edition!

A song has even been written about me by the French band

The Concept, and it was posted on YouTube. The track carries my name and the chorus goes: 'Antoine Griezmann is the man, yes he can!' My sister played it to me and I thought it was funny. That's when you realise you're starting to get famous.

In August 2016, I was also included in the ranking of France's favourite personalities. The newspaper *Le Journal du Dimanche* publishes its top 50 every six months and I went straight into sixth place, between Jean Reno and Sophie Marceau. It's not something I specifically seek but, yes, I'm popular. And I'm proud of it. Of course I benefit from the influence of the France team, which is powerful. This is also why we are careful in what we say because headlines can be generated from not very much. *Les Bleus* give you a power, and it is our job to make French people happy.

I certainly feel like I've changed in the eyes of others. Everything has happened so suddenly. When I was 18 and wearing the colours of Real Sociedad, it was me who would ask an opponent to swap shirts. Now it's the other way around. I note that I'm the favourite player of some of the other players' children. That's a sign, as is the fact that referees today call me by my name or that fans shout my name as soon as I get off the coach.

Another way of measuring my fame is by counting the number of shirts I have to sign these days when I arrive at France's training base at Clairefontaine. We are given lots to scribble on so they can be given to personalities at various gatherings, and my quota has risen significantly.

It's also nice to be appreciated away from football and recognised just for my personality. When I was 17 or 18 I couldn't stand being stared at all the time, seeing people turn around when I was going to have a drink, as if they were monitoring my alcohol intake. But I recognise that notoriety is nice … though in order to stay popular, you need to remain successful, beginning with the national team. There was the Platini generation, then the Zidane generation. I hope one day there will be the Griezmann generation, to be the player of a thrilling period, the one people will remember in 10 or 20 years. I'm doing everything for that to be so.

The requests I receive are extremely varied. I like to step out of my universe and get away from football, and the Lego Batman animation film allowed me to do that. When Maud told me that the producers wanted me to do the voice of Superman *(1)* I wasn't especially motivated. I was tired. But my sister knew how to find the right words in order to convince me, and I accepted. It was a cool experience.

For the dubbing I had to follow the lines of the text closely and stick to the pictures, which wasn't easy because it was my first experience in this field. Superman's character was very funny, like the film. As I didn't have the time to travel to Paris, the team came to Madrid. The session took part in a studio and I was finished in two-and-a-half hours. I only had two scenes to 'play'.

The cinema has never made any other approaches to me, although I have been asked to appear in a video. I turned it down. I don't have time, so I have to say no to almost everything. This was the case for the Restos du Cœur. I was touched that Les Enfoirés *(2)* wanted me for their filmed concert but the games were piling up and I had to think about my recovery. I passed over the opportunity because I needed to focus. But I hope the chance will come around again. I don't have a great singing talent but if I was with lots of other people, I would know what to do.

Advertising has also given me the chance to get to know other things and go behind-the-scenes. With the former rugby player, Fabien Galthié, I recorded an advert for Sport 2000, a popular family brand in France. I've also done spots for three international companies: Gillette, Beats audio headphones and Puma. I'm with Usain Bolt in one of them, although we never met. Our timetables weren't compatible. We filmed our scenes individually. I learned what I had to do straight away.

In the part, I'm wearing a suit and I'm imitating his famous lightning bolt celebration on the same evening that he's doing mine. The piece was shown worldwide. The other icon of that sports manufacturer is Rihanna: why not film a commercial with her? In Puma's latest offering I went a bit further, playing Cupid for a young couple. There again, my gimmick inspired from the 'Hotline Bling' video by the rapper Drake is helpful. It allows me to be a barman, hairdresser, knitter and even a fighter pilot all at once! I love this form of self-depreciation and I had great fun on the set, where everything was shot against a green background. I have never taken acting lessons.

The only downside to this? The six hours of filming. I'm not a very patient person! The director loved to do loads of takes; towards the end I made him understand that I wanted things to move more quickly.

I get contacted by many brands. I choose them according to what they mean to me. I've also got to feel good about the people I'd be working with. I have already turned down very lucrative offers because I didn't agree with what they were trying to get across. My motives are not just financial. There is no way I would just do anything.

That's not to say I don't have any favourites. This was reflected when I was approached by Ruban Blanc *(3)* which campaigns against violence towards women. Usually it takes a month or two for a filming date to be arranged. But here the script was sent to me and the meeting arranged for the following week with the Kering Foundation *(4)*.

In the video I play the part of a spokesman for women who have been mistreated, reading the testimony of a young lady who had been abused when she was a girl. We footballers, while we're just kicking a ball, have the power to reach out to many people. Why should we not do this when it comes to supporting noble causes? That said, I don't go near politics. Firstly because you shouldn't mix things and then because the subject holds absolutely no interest for me, at least for now. Sometimes in Spain or France I'm introduced to members of the government; I don't know who they are. I watch very little television.

After the Brazil World Cup in 2014, I relied on the 4Success management agency, created by Sébastien Bellencontre in association with Farid Boumkais, to help me sort through everything and help me with sponsors who fit in with my values. I broke off from them at the start of 2017 to go with my sister.

I also have a community manager, André de Sousa. He is valuable because I am active on social media. Today I have 6.7 million people following me on Facebook, 3.4 million followers on Twitter and 8.4 million on Instagram. André is a childhood friend. He didn't play much football but he used to come to my grandmother's house. We lost touch with each other when I left Mâcon.

One day, I stumbled across my Facebook page which he had launched. Being an administrator he took care of it on his own. I congratulated him on what he had done. We have since resumed contact and we have forged links again. He has since developed my other profiles, which he faithfully keeps up to date.

André works for the town of Mâcon, in the communication department, where he also manages social media. He takes care of mine for free. He has never asked for a penny. He could have come to me for money but he hasn't. He has even refused it when I've offered it to him. Sometimes I just pay his plane tickets so he can visit me. He is a real mate.

I do my own Twitter and Instagram stuff, even though he can serve as an intermediary. I laugh, I joke, I take photos. There are even a few mistakes: it's really me! He is Facebook. We communicate a lot on that. On the networks, where a large community still follow me, I don't filter things. I share my feelings, my emotions. I am not trying to sell anything and if I have to refer to a commercial sponsor then I'm satisfied with doing the minimum. I am on the Web as I am in life.

My dad gets lots of requests for shirts and photos, and that causes disagreement between us. I don't want him to say yes to everybody.

In Mâcon, some people would insist a bit too much. They'd swear they had been at primary school with his son or whatever. It never ends. I told him he couldn't make everyone happy, giving out shirts and photos hand over fist. I don't want people taking advantage of him or abusing his kindness.

Obviously giving presents and making people happy is important. But there comes a time when one has to preserve oneself, protect oneself.

Not long ago, my dad took me to the airport and inside the door of the car I spotted a huge bunch of pictures of me which, I guess, he hands out so he can make kids happy. He doesn't know how to say no. Sometimes some people need to have 'no' said to them!

I have many women among my admirers. Am I aware of the sex appeal I give off? Yes, but I don't play on that. I'm not into trying to look good on the field or elsewhere.

I receive many letters and even gifts for my daughter or myself, even when we have an away game. Each day four or five letters arrive at Atlético's headquarters. I don't often reply, otherwise I'd spend my days doing this. That said, I read everything.

I have even received a marriage proposal! It came from a little four-year-old girl. She wrote this to me: *Hello, my name is Capucine and I am four! I have made you a pretty necklace. Lots of kisses, Capucine. P.S. I wanted to marry you but my mum says I'm too little.*

I found that message very cute, even though her mum no doubt helped her and I showed it to Erika in the kitchen. I posted this reply on my Twitter account: *Capucine, know that I received your letter and I adore your necklace. Thanks to my Team Grizi for all your messages.*

Of course, temptations do exist. A footballer is an easy prey: someone who is young, who earns money and is impressionable.

When I took my first steps in the professional world, I saw more and more girls hanging around players. But that wasn't an issue for me: I had what I needed at home!

I am faithful in friendship and in love. I wasn't looking for a one-night stand, but for a person of trust with whom I could build a relationship and take things easy. I knew that, with Erika, I would be better on the field. I understood very quickly that she would be the woman in my life, the one with whom I wanted to live and have a child.

(1) in the French version of Superman.

(2) The name given to the singers and performers in the yearly charity concert for the Restaurants du Cœur, the French charity which distributes food packages and hot meals to those in need.

(3) White ribbon.

(4) Combats violence against women.

6

SON OF SPAIN

France gave birth to me. But Spain has adopted me. Erika, Mrs. Griezmann, is Spanish, I swear in Spanish, I encourage myself on the field with 'vamos, vamos' and my friends are Iberian, apart from two or three I've kept from my childhood in Mâcon. In Spanish the words just come out naturally, spontaneously. I even speak to my dog, Hooki, a French bulldog, in that language. When my daughter was born I only spoke to her in Spanish. It was more natural for me, even though I am trying hard to get Mia to master French as well. I've lived like a Spaniard since my teenage years. This country has done everything possible to make me feel like one of its own.

Obviously the settling in came through football. Since arriving at Real Sociedad I have done loads of toros, the collective exercises where you have to keep the ball in a confined area. I devoured the ball every day. I could feel the improvement I was making. I had been slow when I came, but I began to become more lively, less self-conscious. My game developed through repeated one-touch play. My technique was more refined. I was able to anticipate, I was guessing before the others were and when the ball was going to come. That culture was essential. Youth development in Spain is a philosophy, a state of mind. When we played in training we were only allowed one or two touches of the ball before getting rid of it. It was a lot to get to grips with, having to think before receiving the ball. The daily repetition of these same drills eventually made it something you would do automatically.

I think I am currently among the world's best at first time play, and I owe that to Real. Anyway, I have never been a dribbler, including when I used to play for fun with my friends in Mâcon. I would play a little deep, so I could see more of the game.

My rise in the Basque Country was both methodical and natural. At first I trained every day after school, from 6.30pm. I only thought about football. One day Éric Olhats asked if I'd like to be a ballboy for a season in the games at the Anoeta. I gladly accepted: it meant I could watch the pros as close as was possible, gauging the fervour of a stadium from the touchline, while taking in the atmosphere and experiencing the same emotions as the senior players.

I had the opportunity to do this when Real Madrid came. It was the team of the Galacticos, with Zidane, David Beckham, Ronaldo, Raul and Roberto Carlos. I was so proud to put my kit on in the dressing room and we were all given a ball. I was fascinated by this team of stars. Rather than watching my own team warm-up, I only had eyes for Real and my idol Beckham.

As soon as the game was finished, I jumped over the fence and rushed to Zidane. I asked him for his shirt but I hadn't seen that he had already swapped it with an opponent. On seeing my disappointment he said: "Follow me." That's exactly what I did. We went down the stairs which led to the dressing room and I went with him into the bowels of the stadium. I thought he was going to offer me a picture or an autograph or whatever. But no: Zidane handed me the shorts he had just been playing in. I couldn't believe it!

I carried out ballboy duties for quite a few games that season. I was excited as I dissected the action, imagining myself scoring and marking the goal with an original celebration. The game would be over too quickly. As had been so with Real Madrid, it was a big thing when Barcelona came. They too had some big hitters with Xavi, Andrés Iniesta, Lionel Messi, Deco, Ronaldinho and Samuel Eto'o. There was also one brilliant French player: Ludovic Giuly. I managed to get hold of the top he wore in the warm-up. The players were decent and approachable, and I could relate to them. That is why, even today, I respond to people who ask me for an autograph or a picture. I was just like them not so long ago.

Back then my dream was to one day play a game for Real Sociedad. I didn't look any further than that. When I went past the Anoeta, this elegant arena, I would think: "That will be my stadium. I want to score goals there."

I began to train with the reserves. I generally operated as a playmaker, a sort of number 10. The former Real Sociedad striker, Meho Kodro, who even played a year for Barcelona, had been coach of his native Bosnia-Herzegovina before taking charge of our reserve team. He liked me a lot. He enjoyed my skill but found me frail. He only showed me a moderate amount of confidence and made me play with people a year younger than me.

The turning point came on the day I had been invited to

join in with the first team. I was in the hallway of the Zubieta training complex after finishing a session. This was July 2009, when I was 18. Suddenly I heard Éric Olhats in the distance and he said to me: "I need to talk to you, Toine. It's very important!"

To be honest, deep down I was thinking: "Right, he's going to tell me something which I'm really going to need to know such as 'wait for me in the car when you're done'... as if I was going to do the trip from Zubieta to Bayonne, which is over 60 kilometres, by bike! I went up to him and to my great surprise he was smiling from cheek to cheek as he told me that I'd be training with the first team that afternoon. What a fantastic feeling that was! It was a dream. Rubbing shoulders with the Chilean goalkeeper, Claudio Bravo, who went on to play for Barça and Manchester City, or the Spanish midfielders Mikel Aranburu and Xabier Prieto: all these players whose performances I used to watch so closely every weekend on television, on EITB, the Basque Country channel which broadcast all the games.

When I got on the field, I was slightly out of things, with two or three reserve players. It was pre-season and the whole squad wasn't there. I wasn't surprised to be put to one side. I thought that was natural. Pros shouldn't have to mix with young players, at least not before a period of adjustment.

The coach was new: a Uruguayan, Martin Lasarte. As a defender with Nacional Montevideo, he won the Copa Libertadores and the Intercontinental Cup. Since becoming a coach he had operated most of the time in South America, from Uruguay (Atlético River Plate) to Colombia (Millonarios) and in his homeland again at Nacional Montevideo, where he notably set his compatriot Luis Suarez on his way.

The coach told us that we were going to play a small training match. It couldn't have been better for me: I love that. Because the Colombian left winger, Jonathan Estrada, had got injured that morning, Lasarte put me where he usually played. I looked up towards the stands to make sure he was watching, looking for a sign. From far away I saw him give the thumbs-up. It was green for go. It was up to me to make the most of it. I showered in the reserves' dressing room at the end of training. Then I went to look for Éric in his office. Instead of talking, as he usually did, about what I had done well or badly, we looked at each other without saying anything. Then we smiled. We were thinking the same thing: "What's happened to me today is totally crazy!"

The return to Bayonne was completed around 10pm, like most of the time. Again, it was classic stuff on the agenda: cook as quickly as possible in order to sleep and recuperate. Then a phone call interrupted the daily routine. Éric's phone rang the moment we reached the apartment. No panic, once again it was probably a French agent offering him a player for Real. But he started the conversation in Spanish and I understood it was the club calling him. He hung up and revealed to me: "Good news. Tomorrow at ten o'clock you'll be training again with the first team!" I burst with joy. I quickly went to bed so I could be in the best condition for the following morning. I had other sessions with the pros, benefiting from one or two injuries and from the fact that others were still on holiday and also because the coach wanted new blood.

The time had arrived for my first friendly game. I've forgotten who the opponents were. Lasarte named me in his squad. Obviously I had only one desire: to play. I started off on the bench. I imagined that the coach had picked two teams and that I'd be in the second one. However, ten minutes before the break the pressure increased: all the substitutes began warming up, and I was among them. The referee blew for half-time. The players who had began the match returned to the dressing room while we kept things ticking over until our fitness coach, Pablo Balbi, told us to listen to Lasarte's team talk. It was there, on the board in the dressing room, that I saw the number 11 and my name. I was going to start the second half. I couldn't believe my eyes. I, Antoine Griezmann, from Mâcon, was getting ready for my first match with Real Sociedad's professional team…

I scored two goals in that half: one with the right, the other with the left. I was warmly congratulated by the dressing room, including the captains and the team's top players. After showering, the fitness coach set out the agenda for the next day. Looking at the players he said, pointing to one after the other: "You, ten o'clock tomorrow with us. You, with the reserves." When he came to me he asked: "You? Hang on, I'm going to ask." In my mind my thoughts were all over the place. I was hoping, praying, that he would keep me again. *'Please, coach, pick me, pick me…'* Balbi came back with his answer: "You, at ten tomorrow with us."Yes! I had managed to catch the coach's eye. I was aware of the huge opportunity which had come my way. There was absolutely no way I was going to stop now.

I played in the friendlies which followed and, with six goals in five games, two of which were braces, I finished top scorer in pre-season. I began to integrate into the team and feel better and better. I was carving out a place for myself, and I was given a locker with the pros. I knew I couldn't take anything for granted and that, in football more than anything else, everything can go quickly in either direction. I had to keep working tirelessly and prove that I deserved my place. But my ambition of starting the season with the first team remained intact. I skipped a level, moving directly from the juvenile ranks to knocking on the door of the first team.

We opened the season with a trip to the Canaries. On August 28th, 2009, Las Palmas were our opponents at the start of the Liga Adelante, the second division. I didn't come on. The others who were like me stayed to train on the field. I went in goal to relax, diving to pull off saves. I didn't take myself too seriously. I was simply enjoying the moment.

On September 2nd, we played host to Rayo Vallecano, another Madrid club also in the second division, in the King's Cup. I watched the game from the bench, like a privileged spectator, when the fitness coach tossed a green bib onto my legs. I looked right and left so as to convince myself that he was, in fact, throwing it to me. He handed out three bibs to the players who had a chance of coming on at any time. *"Vamos, Antoine, dale a calentar,"* ("Right, Antoine, go and warm up,") he ordered.

While I was warming up, I was watching the game and also looking at the fitness coach, seeing if he was signalling in my direction. I couldn't bear it, flying up and down the touchline. Then Lasarte called Pablo Balbi, who began to hurry towards him. He came over and announced the first change: *"Griezmann, entras tu en cinco minutos!"* ("Griezmann you're on in five minutes!") The pressure...

I accelerated my warm-up, and went back to the bench to listen to the coach's instructions. "Play as if you were in the street with your mates," he urged. I was positioned in midfield, the fourth official inspected my studs and made sure I was wearing my shin-pads. I waited for the ball to go out before coming on. It took five minutes for that to happen, five very long minutes, as if the ball was deliberately delaying my entrance. Finally, the referee blew for a throw-in. I am coming on for my first official game. Number 27, Antoine Griezmann.

As soon as I step onto the pitch I'm given a mini ovation, which makes me feel warm inside. I am one more player from the *cantera* – the club's development scheme – who has made it into the first team. I didn't have many touches of the ball. But my first one filled me with the kind of adrenalin which I get only when I score. After a rebound I pressed my opponent into heading the ball to me. I'm in the centre circle with, alongside me, the last opposing line of defence. I go on a long run. The fans are carrying me along. I've got shivers. I'm galvanised so much by the supporters that I find myself faced with the keeper. But I've got a pinch of stress and I push the ball too far on my left. I feel all alone. I manage to get my shot in. Unfortunately, the keeper knocks it for a corner with his legs. But the fans have been able to get to know me! It would have been so wonderful to score in my first official match, which happened to end in defeat.

Four days later I figured in a second division game. It was at home again, on match day two, and I came on against Murcia for the last quarter of an hour. It finished goalless. I played the following week against Gimnàstic de Tarragona. Lasarte put me on for the last minute, to break up the rhythm and to waste time and ensure victory. A week later, against Gijón at the Anoeta, the coach sent me on at half-time along with another striker, Imanol Agirretxe. We were losing but we were able to get an equaliser.

The most notable moment of my young career comes on September 27th, 2009. During the week I didn't know if I was going to be playing or not. The coach alternated between Jonathan Estrada, with whom I had become pally, and me. On the day of the match, at home against Huesca, Lasarte informed me that I was going to start. My first time as a first choice! Once again he tells me to play without pressure and to do exactly as I had been doing in training. That's easier said than done…

It's impossible to have the same kind of siesta as a player who has played 100 games in La Liga. Of course, I couldn't sleep. Even these days I hardly get a siesta on match days. In order to cut myself off I prefer to watch a TV series or play video games. I was tense when the team entered the field. Not really at ease. Then the referee blew for kick-off. It was like a release. I tried to gain confidence from my first few touches, without complicating things. Even so I did attempt a dribble or a forward pass.

In the 40th minute, I took a pass from Mikel Aranburu near the penalty area. I controlled the ball with my left and then moved it to my other foot. So I asked myself: "What am I doing? Don't go on your right foot!" I finally let fly with a right foot shot which floated from outside the box, and I could sense it was going in. The ball hit the net. Damn! What do I do now? Instinctively, I went to celebrate my goal by running towards the stands, my arms apart. I kissed the club badge. Tears were in my eyes. I pulled on my shirt, making sure the fans could see it, and I shouted "Vamooooos!"

The Griezmann footballer was definitely born that day. I thought of all those mornings where I would go past the Anoeta by car, assuring Éric loads of times: "That, that is my stadium. I'm going to play there and score lots of goals!" What's more, against Huesca, I scored with my right foot, if you please … I will never forget it. My goal meant I kept my place in the team. It also showed the coach that he could trust me. I was beaming in the dressing room, and I experienced the joy of my team-mates, who were genuinely happy for me, the blond, shy French guy who was always smiling. I couldn't wait to play again and to score.

Overall, I played in 37 of our 42 League games. After scoring against Cadiz in the 90th minute I dived into the snow which had been piled up on the touchline! I scored six goals in total, the second highest tally. Real Sociedad were crowned Second Division Champions, ahead of Hercules, Levante and Real Betis. In the wake of that I signed my first professional contract.

People were beginning to talk about me, fans wore shirts with my name on. It didn't go to my head. I didn't read the newspapers – I still don't – and the San Sebastián club protected me by keeping me away from media pressure. I was in a cocoon. Everything had been put in place for me to concentrate solely on football. Lasarte used me intelligently. I appreciated him greatly, he said the right things. There was a period when I wasn't so good on the field, a bit out of sorts in training. So the coach decided not to pick me against Albacete. He took me to one side the next day and let rip: "I hope you'll feel good about not playing. You're not at it right now, I'm not seeing any desire to improve." He was right to have a go at me. He used to speak to me a lot and explain the things that were wrong…

Away from football, I was also beginning to find my independence. I was no longer staying at Éric's. I was living in an apartment near Saint-Sebastián, which was more practical. The club paid the rent. Initially I had been put up by a team-mate, Emilio Nsue López, who was at Real Sociedad in our promotion year, on loan from Mallorca, where he was born. He was barely two years older than me but he was already in a relationship, his girlfriend being a bit older. I stayed a few months with them. They spoiled me. Emilio used to take me on the ten-minute drive to training. He would wait for me after the sessions at Zubieta. I had my own room and I often played on the PlayStation. I was like their child, Emilio's girlfriend waited on me hand and foot.

I then shared an apartment with another team-mate, Javi Ros, who was almost a year older than me. Very quickly I felt the need to be alone. The beach of La Concha, which is a kilometre-and-a-half stretch of white sand, wasn't far away. In the summer I also enjoyed jumping among the rocks in Biarritz. Naturally I was speaking perfect Spanish by then, but I had a little more difficulty with Basque. At first, when they were laughing in that language in the dressing room, I thought they were making fun of me.

I got my first tattoo when I was 18. I wanted one which shows and which reflects my personality. I looked around, and it was my team-mate and friend Liassine Cadamuro-Bentaïba, who found the phrase on the Internet which suited me. It is from the writer Antoine de Saint-Exupéry: *Make your life a dream, and a dream a reality.* I chose it because it expresses the difficulties and the pain you go through in order to make it. Yes, I went through hell! This saying is my guide.

That tattoo accompanies the one of the Virgin Mary, to whom my mum often prays. She is a devout Catholic. Through her influence I have been religious since I was very small. I used to go with her to church to light a candle. I showed the same expression of faith when I was in Real Sociedad's junior teams, begging for help so I could turn professional or when things got difficult. I still like to light candles in churches from time to time.

In June 2015, when I was in Paris to celebrate my brother Théo passing his bac *(1)*, I went with Erika to Sacré Cœur. I wrote a few words in the visitors' book, asking the Lord to take care of my family, to keep us healthy and to thank him for bringing Erika into my life. I don't pray every day, but sometimes I feel the need, especially the night before games. A football dressing room is a place where everyone comes together, in a brotherhood, with all the religions.

I room on my own in the France team. With my Xbox! When I knock on Paul Pogba's door and he doesn't answer, I know it's because he's praying, so I go away and leave him alone. Ditto when he gets out his mat. I like watching him. I find it interesting to compare our respective practices. When we have people around for a barbecue I make sure I choose the right kind of meat for when we are expecting Muslims.

I thrive on all the faiths. There is no environment more diverse than football. In the absence of tourism, our away trips tell us a lot about this aspect, and about the various cultures which exist in the countries where we play. For example, Coca-Cola isn't the same in Russia. In Spain the steak haché doesn't have the same taste. I think that the good taste of minced meat is what I miss most about France! When I go back to Mâcon my little steak is waiting for me.

Going back to tattoos, I had some others done after the one of the Virgin Mary, from Christ the Redeemer, which dominates Rio – which I got before going to Brazil, not knowing that I'd be playing in the World Cup – to my parents' initials on an anchor, and to clouds and a rosary. I have also got the letters H.O.P.E written on my fingers. I had wanted tattoos for ages, but I waited until I was older.

My parents didn't try to talk me out of getting them. My mum would have found it hard to stop me: she's got some herself. The first was put behind her right shoulder, representing my dad's star sign in Chinese. Even he gave in to it years ago, when he had our first names and the date of his marriage done. Maud also has some. I have no idea whether Théo will get any. I've had the same tattoo artist from the start. He lives in Saint-Sebastián and if I can't find the time to get over there I bring him to me. There is still some room on my arms!

By the time I had my first car I still hadn't got my driving licence. It was a blue Scirocco R. I had spoken to my parents before buying this fairly powerful Volkswagen Coupé. I need their opinion when it comes to making a substantial outlay, and that is still the case today. It took me three times to pass my test! I wasn't very good, just like at school. Until I got that pink paper of confirmation it was a team-mate, Gorka Elustondo who drove it.

I got my licence four months afterwards. I then changed cars, opting for a black Range Rover. I only kept it a year before passing it on to my dad. I drove a Maserati GranTurismo for almost two years. Today I use the club's 4x4 as well as two jewels: a white Rolls Royce and a McLaren 675LT, which is also white. I hesitated several months between this rare model and a vintage American car. I consulted Erika and my dad, who told me: "Do what makes you happy."

So finally I treated myself to this present at the end of 2016 as a reward for my good season – though I remain discreet and I don't want to go on about it. I don't go out in Madrid in the McLaren. I use it generally to get to training. I try not to spend money on just anything.

Besides, I need to protect myself. My house is a sanctuary. A newspaper will never make me pose there for a family photo. I want people to carry on seeing me as a normal person, which I am, even though I have become 'bigger'. While I may own some speed machines, I still have a soft spot for my Scirocco R. I remember very well the first time Erika got inside. She loved it and she still speaks to me about it. It's there that we got to know each other…

Erika is in charge. I call her *la jefa* (the boss)! At home she's taken care of everything, from the décor to the layout of the rooms. She is the lady of the house, she knows where all the papers, contracts and all my stuff have been filed. I am, however, in charge of the barbecue. I've just had one put in on the patio. I have raised my game since being with her. I have improved all round. I am a different person, a better man and a better footballer. If I am to be better on the field I also need to be so in my private life. I have been happy ever since I began living with her. I now know that someone is waiting for me at home and I am always in a hurry to get home to her. On a more selfish note, it's thanks to her that I stopped eating frozen ready meals or those made in restaurants!

I met her one summer. When I was playing in the second division I used to train in the mornings and then have lunch in a place which was also open to university students. Erika, who had a degree in teaching, was working towards a licence so she could become a child psychologist. She would go on to do a masters in interior decorating in Madrid. We all used to eat in the cafeteria, me after training with Real Sociedad, she after her course at university. I was sitting down when I saw her come in, but I was hooked immediately. It was love at first sight, but it wasn't (yet) reciprocal.

I asked my team-mates if they knew her. They told me that this young Spanish girl, Erika Choperena, who was my age, was studying here. She came there to eat at lunchtime and in the evening and she slept in the neighbouring boarding school. I watched her for a year and a half, I got closer to her, I sent her messages and I tried to win her over. I worked really hard and I hung in there. And finally I managed to go out with her. We have been together since December 27th, 2011.

I feel good with her, comfortable. We laugh a lot together. She does everything to make me feel fulfilled. Like me, she really likes to be at home. Even though I don't speak a lot and I don't express my feelings much, her presence is both reassuring and soothing. The reason I'm good on the pitch is because, thanks to her, I can concentrate only on football. That's all I need to think about. She attends almost all my games when we're at home. She knows I like it when she's there. I say hello to her with a look during the warm-up.

She produced a fashion blog, 'Cordialmente Erika,' (*'Yours, Erika'*) where she would post her looks, fashion tips or recipes. While some people were encouraging, many, because of my fame, used to leave messages that were insulting or mocking. She was affected by that, and out of concern but also discretion, she chose to close down her account a year later.

I get on very well with her parents. They have done everything to make me feel at ease. They decided to learn French so they could converse with my family. Erika did the same thing. I tip my cap to them! That's the test of true love.

(1) Baccalauréat. The French equivalent of A-levels.

7

BEND IT LIKE BECKHAM

I don't know if I'll ever wear the shirt of Manchester United. Throughout the history of that club some wonderful players have worn the number seven: George Best, Bryan Robson, Eric Cantona, Cristiano Ronaldo and David Beckham. Five Red Devil icons. But for me it's the blond-haired playmaker who represents the club best of all.

His magical right foot was made for United, with whom he won one Champions League, two FA Cups and six league titles. Captain of England and picked 115 times, the 'Spice Boy' also played for Real Madrid, Los Angeles Galaxy and AC Milan before finishing at Paris Saint-Germain.

This midfielder was a true pop star of football. Through his looks and his manner, he was also prized in the worlds of fashion and advertising. And he's my absolute role model. He is the only one I would have loved to play with, even if, these days, watching Mesut Özil is also a delight.

I have always found Beckham to be perfect, both on the pitch and off it. There was a charisma and class about everything he did. He was elegant on the field and in life, and he always dressed well. When it comes to maintaining his image, he's the best. I aspire to be like him, to be comfortable and effective in both domains, knowing how to win trophies and to generate attention.

Beckham is a marketing phenomenon who has become a brand, which I am not yet. Wherever he goes in the world people go crazy. It would be a blast to meet him, even though I don't speak good English. But I imagine he can get by in Spanish, after having spent four seasons at Real. I would like to get to know him, maybe shoot a commercial with him. That would be awesome. He seems like a cool kind of guy, someone who is uncomplicated, despite his status. Kevin Gameiro played with him at Paris and David used to quietly go to the players' barbecue with his wife, Victoria.

I wear the number seven on my back for Atlético Madrid, just as I do for France. It's in homage to David Beckham. And the reason I have always worn long sleeves is also because I want to be like him. I used to find this style chic. When I was playing for Real Sociedad in the second division, I was asked which number I wanted.

In Spain, until you have your professional licence the lowest number you can wear is 25. I said I wanted 71, which is the département of the Saône-et-Loire, the administrative centre of which is Mâcon. That wasn't possible because the number was too big.

The kit man began to list the numbers which were available and I quickly stopped at 27. At least there was a seven in there, like with Beckham! When Real got promoted the person who used to wear the seven left, so I took advantage. And I kept it right to the end. Once I moved to Atlético I went after it again. It was free. Good.

I am the number seven. I like it, it brings me luck. When it came to *Les Bleus*, I started out wearing 11. The seven belonged to Franck Ribéry, who I only played with for a few minutes in my first game. Because of an injury to his lower back, he had to miss out on the World Cup in Brazil. Before inheriting it, I thought it best to send him a message asking if it bothered him. I mentioned it to France's kit man, who spoke about it to Didier Deschamps. The coach said I could have it. Yohan Cabaye was also interested but he kindly left it to me.

In 2015/2016, Atlético Madrid figured among the top ten clubs for worldwide sales of shirts. Almost two million of them were sold, even before the Champions League final. From a personal point of view, I also made the list *(1)*. I'm not really aware of what that means but I'm delighted that more and more people in stadiums choose to have my name put on their piece of fabric. But I'm still after more. Having them buy a shirt with Griezmann on the back is an ambition and a pleasure which I seek. When I see children who have names of others, deep down I say to myself: "I want them to wear my shirt instead. Show them something on the field which makes them want to buy it!"

A shirt is not a trivial thing. I have kept some of the main ones which I've worn. They are at my parents' house in Mâcon. For example there are those of the 2014 World Cup, the one I wore for my official presentation at Atlético, the one where we secured promotion to the first division with Real Sociedad and the one in which I scored a goal against Lyon in the qualifying round of the Champions League. I also brought back Marco

Reus' jersey from the World Cup. He had wanted to swap after our 1-0 defeat by Germany, even though he hadn't played because of injury. I didn't have the heart to swap the shirt from our Euro 2016 final. Most of my shirts are framed in a dedicated room. Maybe one day, when my career is over, it will be a mini museum? Beckham's jersey would be most welcome!

It was his arrival in London for the opening ceremony of the 2012 Olympics which made the biggest impression on me. He had arrived at the stadium in a speedboat sailing on the Thames, with the famous Olympic flame by his side. On the boat and in his impeccable suit, his hair didn't move a muscle. Like Beckham, I like to change my hairstyle. It's a form of signature. I must have tried them all, from the Mohican to Pavel Nedved's blond mop.

When I was 16 I met up with my team-mates at the airport after two days of rest in Mâcon, and I turned up with braids! On seeing my hair stuck to my skull, Éric Olhats burst out laughing and asked what I had done. "Real Sociedad aren't going to like that!" he warned me. He wasn't wrong. We were about to play the USA in a friendly when the coach asked me to change my appearance. "You can't play looking like that. It's not good for the image." Naturally I apologised. I couldn't really understand how something like that could shock, but I did what I was told.

Having a good image is paramount for Real. This wasn't my first original haircut. I haven't been ashamed of any of them, I take full responsibility for them all. Why should I have regrets? I liken it to a tattoo. It's done on impulse. I do it because I want to. Of course, I mull it over before going ahead, but I don't shilly-shally.

On the field as well as off it, David Beckham had a smile.

There again, without forcing the issue, I go about things the same way. Of course, being a footballer is my profession, but first of all it's my pleasure, my passion. Smiling is the least I can do. It's the way I am. It costs nothing to smile. In that respect I am sometimes portrayed as the ideal son-in-law. It's rather enjoyable. On the other hand, I don't like it at all when I'm referred to as the 'anti-Benzema'. It bothers me. It's only in France where people have a go at him. They don't know the true character of Karim, who remains a great player with whom I have always had a good relationship in the France team.

Smiling represents power. It's a weapon. I automatically put one on for a photo. I find it an elegant and polite thing to do, even when I'm not necessarily in a good mood. I think about the person who has asked for the photo; I want them to be happy. Bringing joy to people is part of our job. Besides, generally speaking, football is lacking in smiles. On the field, players are sometimes too tense, too serious. Some of them believe they are something they're not. Yes, football is too serious. Perhaps it's because of what is at stake, but this is not a reason. For example, in the NBA it is customary to have a joke before games, but it doesn't stop you fighting to the bitter end on the court.

It's a matter of personality, but I like to make things more relaxed and bring some atmosphere. Even though people think I'm nice and there's a certain shyness about me when I'm faced with a microphone, I'm actually a bit of a joker. Paul Pogba snitched on me! *(2)*

Publicly at least, it's tricky to joke around in the France team because we are constantly monitored, almost spied upon. At Clairefontaine we have to restrain ourselves from saying or doing something, for fear of what the press or the supporters might think. It's a shame. We are afraid of other people's opinions. On a long training camp with *Les Bleus*, I would love to be able to escape to a restaurant, to the cinema or to the theatre.

In 2015, as a one off, before two matches against Belgium and Albania, we went to a show at the Jamel Comedy Club. I laughed a lot and everyone had a great time. This kind of thing doesn't happen enough. I have never spoken to the coach about it. I'm not big enough in this team to demand this and that. And so we stay cooped up because everything we say can be wrongly interpreted, and we are not always ourselves. We cut ourselves off from people so that we can focus. But we get bored at 'Le Château', most of the time locking ourselves in our rooms.

One Sunday I went to the race track at Vincennes and then to the AccorHôtels Arena, formally known as Bercy, to watch the World Handball Final because I do follow other sports. I wanted people to know that. We often find ourselves confined in our world. With Atlético we took gifts to children in hospital, and I celebrated Chinese New Year in one of the academies, aware that Wanda, a Chinese conglomerate, owns 20 per cent of the club.

I work in a simple, natural way. But I complain when I feel the need to. An example of this was after 'Griezmann's Anxiety' appeared on the front page of *L'Équipe* on June 13th, 2016, following the first Euro 2016 game against Romania. I didn't like that.

I didn't think it was fair, especially after just one match. I felt sick. So did my parents. I knew full well that I hadn't begun the Euros well, but I didn't need this front page, especially as

I had just lost a Champions League final, which was already a mental blow. I spoke to the people concerned at the next media gathering and I told them how cheesed off I was to read that. Conversely, I loved it when, three months later, the same paper brandished 'Vote Griezmann' on its cover, about the Ballon d'Or. That touched me. And I let them know it through a personal message. It was good for me that the whole country got behind me, encouraging me to keep working and to keep the momentum going.

By encouraging *Les Bleus*, the press gives us confidence. Abroad they are totally behind their national team. In France people look for the slightest thing. It's as if they're not pleased that so-and-so is doing well.

In Holland, in October 2016, Paul Pogba scored the only goal of the match with a powerful shot. Even though I had only played a very average game, I was delighted for him. I was truly pleased and I said it over and over again in interviews.

"Tomorrow, he's going to make the front page," I explained. "It will do him good." I hoped he would have the support of the journalists. Paul, who had just arrived at Manchester United, was constantly criticised. We have to support one another. I am, in any case, resolutely positive. Like David Beckham…

(1) 490,900 Griezmann shirts were sold for the 2015/16 season, according to the Euromericas Sports Marketing agency.

(2) In the magazine 'So Foot' (May 2016), Pogba stated: "You've got to know one thing … The guy you see in front of the cameras is not the real person! Because he is crazy. He likes African music! He's a dancer, he dances to everything. Grizou is Reggaeton!"

8

REAL WORLD

My first big experience of playing for Real Sociedad in La Liga came on August 29th, 2010. I came on after an hour against Villarreal, replacing Francisco Sutil, shortly after the first goal. Two-and-a-half weeks later, I found myself playing against Real Madrid, who were lining up with Cristiano Ronaldo, Iker Casillas, Pepe, Sergio Ramos, Marcelo, Mesut Özil, Sami Khedira, Angel Di Maria, Gonzalo Higuaín and Karim Benzema. Both of these experiences – the one of playing, and being fielded from the start – were real boosts. But scoring in La Liga was an even better feeling.

On October 25th, 2010, Real Sociedad were playing at home to Deportivo La Coruña on match day eight, in front of a little more than 20,000 spectators. The experienced Joseba Llorente, one of our summer signings along with Raúl Tamudo, the former captain of Espanyol, opened the scoring on the quarter of an hour mark. Before the game I had told the press officer to ensure that the doors of the promotional car, which was parked on pitch side, weren't locked. "Because if I score, I'm getting in," I'd said. My team-mates knew about this but they ribbed me about it, not really believing I'd do it. "You talk too much," they said. "You won't do it. But if you go for it we're getting in the car with you…" In the 70th minute, Carlos Martinez crosses to me. I meet the ball with my head and the Galician keeper is beaten. 2-0 for the *Txuri-Urdin*, which means blue and whites in Basque, which is our nickname.

After the goal, being a man of my word, I signalled my team-mates to follow me. I leapt over the hoardings and headed towards the car which was parked on the athletics track. I got inside and put my hands on the steering wheel. I was in driver's mode, with my team-mates in the passenger seats. Even the captain, Xabi Prieto, was there. This is not something I'll do again, but I don't regret the celebration. In all the euphoria I picked up a yellow card and I left the field in the 82nd minute, milking the ovation at the Anoeta, the stadium which gave me so much happiness.

This first season in La Liga, more technical and faster than I had previously experienced, and with less space, was fulfilling. I played 34 League games from the left side, scoring seven times, including a brace against Sporting Gijón. I also did well against Hercules Alicante, who had David Trezeguet in their ranks, the only 1998 World Cup winner I've come up against. He was an exceptional goalscorer, a real fox in the box with his 171 goals for Juventus and 34 in 71 games for *Les Bleus*. Both of us scored in this match. I asked him for his shirt at half-time. He gave it to me, but after the game I didn't hang about because we had lost.

My fame was beginning to grow. Outside the Anoeta I saw more and more children wearing shirts bearing the number 27 and the name of Griezmann. I was very proud. The public could relate to me: it had been a long time since a young product of the club had burst into the first team and helped it win games. I felt I was being carried along, encouraged, and that people liked my style and my cheerfulness.

Real ended the season in 15th place. A good position for a newly-promoted team, but not good enough for Martin Lasarte to keep his job. It's true that we had to wait until the last game in order to assure our safety, but I am grateful to the Uruguayan coach. He was replaced by a Frenchman, the ex-goalkeeper, Philippe Montanier, who until then had been coaching Valenciennes. He was accompanied by his faithful number two, Michel Troin.

In his first year we stayed up with three games to go. The club's top scorer in La Liga was our signing, the Mexican Carlos Vela, who was on loan from Arsenal. As for me, I scored eight times and made four assists. I began well by scoring in the second game against Barça, who had Messi, Xavi, Iniesta, Cesc Fabregas and David Villa in their team. I signed a year's contract extension in the summer of 2012. Good news: the club took up its option to buy Carlos Vela. It also signed a lively left midfielder, Gonzalo Castro, whom everyone called 'Chori'. He had been champion three times in his country, Uruguay, and had just spent five seasons with Mallorca.

Things didn't gel immediately: we shipped five in the Nou Camp against Barcelona in our first league game, one of six defeats in our opening 10 fixtures. In addition, I picked up a slight injury. Then, very slowly, we started to get things together. And become irresistible.

Real beat Barcelona, the future champions, 3-2 in stoppage time. We also won in Bilbao, at Atlético Madrid and Seville. We gave Valencia a good going over (4-2) and scraped a 3-3 draw against Real Madrid – a game where I scored. We were able to boast an unbeaten run of 15 games, during which I hit five goals. And we ended the season in a blaze of glory. In the final game we defeated Deportivo La Coruña, who dropped into the second division. I scored the only goal. It was a decisive strike: it allowed us to snap up fourth place, which meant the qualifying round of the Champions League. But it wouldn't be with Philippe Montanier, who chose to sign for Stade Rennais.

I enjoyed his training sessions, which were attack-based, with work done in front of goal and on finishing. Michel Troin, his assistant, used to take me to one side regularly during training to help me fine-tune my heading game and my volleying. I appreciate that it helped me improve and make me more skilful.

Philippe also adopted an intelligent attitude after my night-time trip, in October 2012, with the France Under-21 team (of which you will read more later). "Listen," he told me. "I know that what you did was wrong. You're going to go through a lot in France and it's going to be hard. But I want you to know that you are an important player for us. I have a lot of confidence in you." It felt good to hear those words.

The club was amazing with me. It put me in a bubble, far away from controversy. I worked myself hard and tried to present another impression of myself. Philippe didn't put me in storage, so to speak. I did everything to pay him back for the confidence he had shown in me, scoring ten league goals. I wasn't his favourite and I didn't have any privileges just because we shared the same nationality. But he believed in me and he confirmed to me that if I was in form I would play, and that my mission was to help the team win games.

The atmosphere in the team was excellent. We poked fun at each other and we laughed a lot. Without doubt it was one of the reasons for our brilliant run, where only Barça and the two Madrid clubs finished ahead of us.

The Champions League was only a stud's width away. It was a dream for me. With Montanier, along with Michel Troin, having left for Brittany, the Real president, Jokin Aperribay, entrusted team affairs to his other assistant, Jaboga Arrasate, who was only 35 years old.

In a quirk of fate, our final step before experiencing the great thrill of the Champions League was a play-off tie against Olympique Lyonnais, third in Ligue 1. Lyon, 70 kilometres from Mâcon. Lyon, the club which hadn't believed in me. I was 22 years of age and this game at the Stade Gerland would change the perception that people had of me. I may have been known in La Liga – with already more than 150 professional games under my belt – but France still didn't know me well.

The first play-off game was on August 20th, 2013. Beforehand I had spotted where, as a kid, I used to come with my dad to watch Sonny Anderson, Juninho and the others play. I didn't want this to go wrong.

The plan was to play quickly in attack. In the 17th minute Carlos Vela, who had narrowly broken the offside trap, attacks down the left and crosses to the far post. In my black shirt with my bleached head of hair, I fly through the air and score with a great acrobatic volley from just inside the box. Anthony Lopez couldn't do anything about it. I played as if I was in the street with my mates, just getting on with things. I exploded with joy. That goal did me so much good from a mental point of view. The controversial night out in Le Havre with the Under-21s was still fresh in people's minds and some of them in Mâcon had gone to have a go at my dad over my attitude. They were the same people who were hoping I would fail at Gerland. Tough luck for them. When I pulled off my scissor kick, I went over towards my parents: I knew where they were in the stands. I wanted to celebrate this goal with them. I also jumped into Carlos Vela's arms to thank him for his cross.

If you look again at me after my goal, you can see how happy I am. It was a big thing. Scoring at Gerland, in front of my folks, increased my happiness tenfold. In addition, at the start of the second half, the Swiss player, Haris Seferović, who had arrived in the summer from Italy, increased our lead with a powerful shot. It was tough on Alex Lacazette and Clément Grenier, with whom I had won the European Under-19s Championship. Qualification was not quite in the bag but it felt good. I gave quite a few interviews where I talked about my goal. One of which, on the field, happened to be with *BeIn Sports* and under the nose of their pundit, Sonny Anderson.

In the return leg at San Sebastián a week later, Real added to their lead and won 2-0. There we were, officially in the Champions League.

Not being seeded, we find ourselves drawn in a tough but evenly balanced group, where the favourites are Manchester United. The competition begins in September, with a home game against the Ukrainians of Shakhtar Donetsk. It's a solid team, whose captain is the Croatian Darijo Srna. They have some good Brazilians such as Luiz Adriano, Fernando, Douglas Costa and Alex Teixeira.

We dominated the game and created lot of chances. One fell to me after three minutes, Carlos Vela had one which I created, then Rubén Pardo and the captain Xabi Prieto had their opportunities. But nothing goes in. Worse: in the second half, the striker Alex Teixeira fires a double against us on two counter attacks. Vela hits the bar. The highest level is unforgiving. I'm starry-eyed as I make my acquaintance with the Champions League, with its unique ball, magnificent music and the children in the centre circle who hold the canvas which represents the competition, and wave flags. Even today, with plenty of Champions League games behind me, I can't get enough of this special world. The joy is repeated each time. I still dig it. It's still a dream.

For now, I'm learning. The first away trip illustrates this. After the slap in the face in the Anoeta against Shakhtar, we have to get ourselves together in the BayArena against Bayer Leverkusen. Their captain, Simon Rolfes, opens the scoring just before half-time under the watchful eye of the Germany coach, Joachim Löw. Carlos Vela equalises with a penalty at the second attempt with time almost up. We're thinking we've held onto our first point. Except that in stoppage time, Jens Hegeler, who had come on six minutes earlier, wins it for the Germans with a free-kick. Zero points after two matches.

What's more, the Manchester giants are next up. The English play host to us in their Old Trafford lair. This stadium is, for me, the greatest in the world. It's a thing of beauty, and is my favourite stadium along with the Stade Vélodrome in Marseille. I love everything about it: the atmosphere, the architecture, the sensations you have when you step onto the pitch. And on that pitch are some top people: Patrice Evra as captain, David de Gea in goal, Wayne Rooney, Michael Carrick, Nani and Ryan Giggs, who is 39 years of age and older than our coach!

The reality of the challenge in front of us is obvious from the outset: in the second minute, under pressure from Javier

Hernández, Inigo Martinez puts through his own net. Physically United are chewing us up. It's all happening too fast. Nevertheless we get a great opportunity to score. I hit the angle of the goal on a free-kick and, unfortunately, the ball bounces back out. Still not a single point. We are not good enough.

A fortnight later, on November 6th, 2013, it's our turn to host United. It's game on. They dominate us. Robin Van Persie misses a penalty and hits the post, Marouane Fellaini is sent off. But in the end, this 0-0 draw means we won't get whitewashed, and we can still think of going through mathematically at least. Not for long: while once again we have chances, we fall to pieces in Donetsk. The Ukrainians put four past us in the Donbass Arena, thanks to their Brazilians Alex Teixeira, Luiz Adriano and Douglas Costa. They are very quick up front. Our farewell to the Champions League is concluded with another defeat in December of the same year, against Bayer Leverkusen. Ömer Toprak's goal sends them into the round of 16, along with United. It's a tough apprenticeship. But, deep down, I wasn't dejected. I had been dazzled by the whole experience.

Our bread and butter remains La Liga. For my third season in the top flight, I was still played on the left and I was a regular first teamer. I notched goals against Sevilla, Valencia, Almería and Valladolid. Up to December I was on 11 goals in 15 games. I scored 18 times in the whole calendar year, which was the best total by a French player, ahead of Karim Benzema and André-Pierre Gignac. In a few days my ban will be lifted and I will be available for selection again for France. And I'm a believer.

The year 2014 begins with a similar rhythm: a brace against

Elche and a goal and a win against Barcelona. The reward came in March when Didier Deschamps gave me my first cap for *Les Bleus* against Holland. Real Sociedad finished seventh in the table, thereby qualifying for the Europa League. It was no surprise that Cristiano Ronaldo ended up as top scorer with 31 goals, three more than Lionel Messi and four more than Diego Costa. Alexis Sánchez scored 19 times and I was two behind, equal with Karim Benzema.

Despite this, I was starting to become part of the furniture at Real. I felt that I had to try something new in order to reach the next stage. Having a taste of *Les Bleus* also made me aware of this. My contract was up in June 2015 and I wanted a clean break. The negotiations began after the Brazil World Cup. Atlético Madrid, who had just been crowned champions and had narrowly lost the Champions League final to Real Madrid, also lost Diego Costa, who joined Chelsea. They paid the money in my escape clause to sign me.

Leaving the Basque Country was heart-breaking. These people got to know me and accompanied me to the top. I was their child, cheered as soon as I left the field. I know what I owe Real Sociedad. I was an essential part of things, the top scorer and the person with the highest number of shirt sales. A kind of emblem.

I didn't sneak away like a thief. The club got 30 million euros in the transfer, one of the highest fees it had ever received. However, I felt rejected when my departure was announced. I don't condone the insults I received, after I had given everything. They regarded my transfer as treason. In fact, when I later returned to the Anoeta with Atlético, things went badly and I'm not just talking about the defeat. I was heckled in the warm-up and heavily whistled.

I knew I wouldn't exactly be welcomed with flowers. I had announced that if I were to score I wouldn't celebrate my goal. But in some chants people were baying for my death! The ones of "Griezmann muerete!" ("Griezmann die!") were gushing out. I didn't understand. And this hurt all the more because my parents were in the stands. The atmosphere was harsh and heavy. I didn't feel good for two weeks afterwards. Atlético gave me encouragement and got behind me and that helped.

One Sunday at the end of July 2015 I signed a six-year contract, and I had to be officially introduced in Madrid the following Tuesday. I used the Monday to say goodbye to members of the club.

I wanted to organise a press conference to thank everyone, the public in particular. But Real Sociedad refused. The president feared a bad reaction from the supporters and he didn't want to get involved. I didn't listen to him and I went ahead with it all the same. It was important for me to leave with dignity, to address those who had mattered and to shake the hands with the staff one last time. I thanked the local journalists, the medical staff and the players. In short, everybody.

I wasn't able to say goodbye directly to the fans. However, I did send them a thank you letter for always being there for me. I wrote it on my own. Available in French and Spanish on my social networks it read:

> *When I arrived, I was still a young boy, and you opened the doors of your house to me. You were the first and only ones to grant me your trust. It wasn't easy for me at first, but over the years, through hard work and sacrifices, I broke into the first team. Thanks to your unconditional support, I have been able to play in La Liga.*

> *Today, I thank you for everything, for making me grow, for teaching me all these things and for fulfilling my dream: living my passion which is football.*
>
> *I'd like to thank you all, but we'd be here all night, so I thank all the coaches who showed me their confidence and who pushed me. Thanks to all the management team, to all the staff, to the doctors. Thanks also to the journalists for their comments. Thanks to my team-mates and my former colleagues, who allowed me to believe in a real project, be it off the field or on it, and not to take things easy. And, of course, thanks to you fans for your flawless support every day.*
>
> *Having fulfilled all my dreams thanks to this club and played in the first division and Champions League, I needed a new challenge, new difficulties to face. Atlético Madrid gave me this chance. It's an opportunity I wanted to seize, and I couldn't say no. Yes, I won't be wearing the txuri-urdin shirt any more, and I will no longer be living in San Sebastián, but I will never forget anything I have experienced here!*

I concluded in Basque: *Eskerrikasko bihotzez emandako amimo bakoitzarengatik* which means: *I thank you sincerely for every encouragement.* I was deeply genuine.

From coming to San Sebastián before I turned 14, I played five seasons with the first team, scoring 53 goals in 202 games. You don't erase nine years in the Basque Country with just the stroke of a pen.

9

A SPECIAL SURPRISE

To say that I have a very strong relationship with all my family would be a polite understatement. In fact, there is a huge bond between the Griezmanns.

That might seem paradoxical, since I left home just after the age of 13. I had to cut the cord very young so that I could live my professional dream. But did I really cut it? And did I really want to? In my first couple of years at Real Sociedad, after moving from Mâcon to Bayonne, I experienced a deep sadness. I wanted to stay with my folks.

It wasn't just hard for me. My brother Théo is five years younger than me and as far as he was concerned someone had kidnapped his older brother! He wasn't even 10 when I went away. What's more, Maud, who is eight years older than him, left soon afterwards to continue her studies in Lyon. I call Théo *El Loco*, 'the madman'. My premature take-off didn't make our relationship easy at first. Rightly so he regarded me as his big brother. I take my role seriously and I try to give him advice, which he takes, but only occasionally.

We can argue over small things but I love him lots. I used to play a lot with him in the garage when I was small. We laid down a green carpet to make a pitch. We used tents, the ones which pop up in a couple of seconds, as goals. We had a little World Cup football and we were off. We had hours of fun together. The person who scored went in nets. The goalkeeper had to roll the ball on the ground or throw it onto your head and you had to knock it home. Weather permitting we would play outdoors.

Théo is doing the equivalent of a BTEC HND in sales management in Mâcon. It's important he works at it and tries hard, even if I'm not a good example! At 20 he had the soul of an entrepreneur: he created and launched the ready-to-wear sports label GZ Brand. I'm its ambassador but he financed and conceived it. He needs to find his own way in the world and if he needs help I'll be there. He comes to me in Madrid during his holidays. I love having him around. We play on the Xbox or have a game of basketball.

We set each other challenges. He asks me for the shirts of his favourite players. His collection is beginning to look impressive. I've got him those of Robin Van Persie, whom he adores, and Lionel Messi. I also have those of Robert Lewandowski, Cristiano Ronaldo, Neymar, Iniesta, Falcao and Drogba. I had asked my team-mate Diego Godín for the one of his Uruguay team-mate Edinson Cavani, and he accomplished his mission. Théo remains my little brother. He can get anything from me.

My sister Maud also has a special place in my life. She got a BTEC in tourism in Lyon and a tourism and marketing degree in Paris, as well as a degree in PR and events management from the École Tunon. Maud is my big sister, there are three years between us, and even though we initially shared the same bedroom we were quickly separated. She often wasn't there when I used to go back home to Mâcon. We would meet up with each other for the summer holidays. But two or three weeks together is too little time in which to enjoy one another's company. I still don't know her by heart. Today she is very present in my life. I need her.

I asked her to take care of my press relations. So as not to leave anything to chance she went on a course in media communication at the Centre de Formation et de Perfectionnement des Journalistes (CFPJ). She also manages my diary. It gives us an opportunity to call each other very often. She is based in Paris and she comes over to Madrid to see me every two weeks or so, in order to supervise an interview she has organised or take in a photoshoot. So it means I can see her quite regularly.

I admire her greatly. For heaps of reasons. For example, I was in Paris one Sunday to record the Canal Football Club TV show. Maud, of course, was there during the broadcast. With the recording over, she asked me if I wanted her to book a hotel or if I wanted to sleep at hers in the 20th arrondissement *(1)*. "You're mad, I'm coming to yours. That way you can show me your apartment!" I told her, feeling happy. The taxi dropped us off outside her building. We went up on foot to the fifth floor, no lift. I was out of breath just on reaching the landing.

On entering her house I discovered a living room with a kitchenette. There was a small bathroom with bath, she had a washing machine, toilet and a bedroom. In other words it was spartan accommodation. I immediately thought: "Ah, yes, respect for my sister. Your brother is a professional footballer and you live in a tiny flat, yet you haven't asked for anything.

And you are always smiling, happy and on top form. I'm proud of you." I left the next day to join up with the France team at Clairefontaine and I wrote to her everything I thought about her.

I'm thrilled she works for me. In some ways we are regaining our youth. She came with us when I went on holiday to New York. She has a reassuring presence about her. I trust her totally when it comes to dealing with journalists. She sorts everything out and puts forward suggestions. She knows me through and through, she knows when I need time to rest. She can guess just by looking at me if I'm tired or not and when it's time to finish an interview. Sometimes she will eat with journalists or give them a peck on the cheek. I would prefer her to keep her distance, but that's the way she is.

Maud has character. She is very independent and stand-alone and she travels a lot for pleasure. I don't yet have a clear idea of what I will do after football – I've got time to think about that – but one way or another I hope she will be by my side.

My mum cuts a striking figure in the family galaxy. Madre Isabelle. I call her *Ouzbelle*. I can only thank her for all the efforts she made to ensure that her child could fulfil his dream, or at least try to.

When I left for Real Sociedad, nobody knew if I would ever become a professional player. Not my dad, not Éric Olhats, not my mum. And nor did I, of course. We were sailing through a complete haze. Our separation was hard for her to endure, just as it was for me. I know it wasn't easy and because of my absence things would often get complicated between her and my dad. I owe my success to her. For that alone I will be eternally grateful to her!

I have memories of how we'd talk together at home about

what was on my mind and how things were going in Spain. Each day before I was due to leave for Real Sociedad via Bayonne, I'd go and play football with my mates. I'd get home about 5pm. I didn't choose that time randomly: my mum had often prepared pancakes around then! I would also take a big bubble bath. She would come to the edge of the bath tub and we would talk. It was our special time. We would speak two sentences and then we'd end up crying. But it was impossible.

These moments were so hard for us both, nevertheless crying together did us some good. Sometimes my dad tried to talk to us but he wasn't allowed to come into the bathroom. Again, it was our special time.

"What are you doing?" he wondered from behind the door. "Are you all right?" He suspected we were sad. He didn't push it. I am proud of my mum.

I would like to have three children with a small age gap. But on this particular day, when Erika asks me to accompany her to the doctor's, having a baby is certainly not on the agenda. I feel I've still got time, and so I don't think about it. It's a typical week, busy as usual, with daily training sessions, photoshoots and meetings with the press.

After the morning stint with Atlético, Erika wants me to come with her. She has a routine doctor's appointment. Usually I avoid going there. When training is over I prefer to rest at home, whereas at the doctor's I'm going to have to wait, meet people, sign autographs and pose for photos. If I can avoid that in favour of my recovery, I will do. But this time I comply. We enter the doctor's office. The tests are normal. Before we leave she suggests that Erika should have a blood test. Once again I'm to go with her. We'd get the results in a week's time.

As expected, the doctor says that she can pick them up at the hospital. We were walking around Madrid and we went back there together. Erika's gynaecologist hands her the envelope and says: "You're pregnant!" There's a massive silence. We looked at each other for a good minute without being able to say a thing. We were moved, yes, but we didn't know what to think. "Thank you very much, doctor. See you next time," we said to her before leaving.

As soon as we got into the car the questions came thick and fast. Erika was fearful of my parents' reaction. "What will they say? And what do we do?" She couldn't stop asking questions. "What do you think? How do you feel about it?" I didn't have a shadow of doubt. "*Gordi* (that's my nickname for her) if my parents or whoever aren't happy then that's their problem. I'm going to start preparing, and we'll be ready on time." I try to reassure her as much as I can.

We waited three months before telling our parents, enough time to be sure that the fœtus was developing well and the pregnancy would go all the way. Once she was certain about this, Erika made the most of an Atlético away game to return back home to Bera Vera de Bidasoa, a Basque Country village, very near the French border. She couldn't wait to announce her pregnancy. Her parents were especially emotional, her dad unable to hold back his tears.

I just needed to inform mine now. Luckily I've got two days off. It's the chance to go back to Mâcon with Erika, who wanted to be with me when I told my parents that they were going to be grandparents! I admit I was a little stressed out. I get to the house, I put my bags down and I ask them, along with my brother Théo, to wait for me in the lounge. They are all there, without knowing the reason why.

I hand an envelope to each of them. "Here, a little present for you..."

My mum can't wait to take it and open it. She says: "Is that true? Oooooooh, I am so happy!" Then it's my dad's turn. I couldn't hold back my tears. I had placed a scan of our future child in the envelope. These two days off were glorious. My parents and my brother were pleased by the news. Maud wasn't there. I FaceTimed her soon afterwards to tell her, when she was in the car.

After nine months of pregnancy a little girl appeared. Rather, a little princess. She was born on April 8th, 2016. My sister was born on April 7th. My situation was somewhat different, and difficult. My birth was by caesarean section. Erika was trembling with fear and was nervous, which is understandable. She was afraid something would happen to her and to the baby. But thanks to the midwife, I was able to be present with her for the birth. I remember the monitors to my right, showing Erika's heartbeat. I couldn't stop looking at them, feeling helpless. That's when a nurse said to me: "Talk to your wife, say nice things to her."

"I'm not very talkative at the best of times, so you can imagine how I'm feeling!" I replied.

I was also very scared, which is why I kept focusing on the monitors. A few minutes later the baby let out her first cry. It was so beautiful and intense. We put her on Erika so they could start getting to know each other. The hospital staff, who were fantastic, then gave Mia to me so they could tend to Erika. I was alone with MY daughter! I whispered little things to her, which will remain between her and me. Sorry!

At first we had thought about calling her Alba, but then we decided on Mia. We adored that name as soon as we heard it.

Since becoming a dad, which fills me full of joy, there's only one thing I can't wait to do once training is over: go home and make the most of my daughter. I even cut short my massages. I want to enjoy every moment because things go so quickly, especially when you are playing every three days or so.

I don't want my wife and daughter being in the press. I post the occasional photo on Twitter to share with my followers, but no more. If Mia is pictured, you don't see her face. I didn't even reveal her name for several months. My private life must be respected. I am careful with what I say. I also make sure my parents and even my sister and brother don't give too many interviews. I've said the same thing to my mates from childhood.

Mia has already come to see me play. I gave her a little wave when I scored. Like Erika, she has transformed me.

Alain, my father, *el padre*, is the head of the family. He looks after everything, takes care of us, protects me and thinks about my later career. It was he who got me into football and passed on his love for the ball.

When I said yes to Real Sociedad, many people in Mâcon took him for a madman. I know what they thought: "How can he send his son to another country at his age? He forced him to leave home because of football!" They were saying this behind his back. But I was the one who forced him, in a way, to let me go. And, today, the people who used to criticise my dad are now coming to congratulate him on my success.

My dad very rarely expresses what he feels, a bit like me. However, sometimes I do. Not him: he is perpetually calm and enigmatic. But I can tell when he's proud and happy. When we played in Munich for the second leg of the Champions

League semi-final against Bayern, we went through despite losing (1-2). I scored our only goal in the Allianz Arena, which was enough following our first leg win (1-0). The Atlético team and staff all stayed on the pitch at the end to celebrate.

I was looking for my dad in the stands. When I finally found him I ran towards him. I wanted to kiss him and share this moment with him. We gave each other a big hug. I heard him say: "Hey, that's brilliant. You're in the final, son, yeeeessss!" It was so beautiful and rare that I was very emotional.

On the other hand, I advise you not to watch one of my games with him, be it in the stadium or in front of the telly. For a start, the closer the match is the more stressed he gets. It's as if he himself was going to play. He gets annoyed very often during the games. He is twitchy and tense. And he yells at everyone! "Antoine, how can you mess up that pass? No, shoot don't get rid of it! Why doesn't he give it to Antoine? He's got to put it away…"

That's a selection of what he says at home. Théo told me this and he even made a secret recording. It's explosive! Sometimes my dad weeps with joy after a goal. He really is a phenomenon. No doubt he would have loved to be in my place, which is why he is fully committed. He doesn't miss any of my matches. He wants to watch them alone. My mum knows that. It doesn't bother her: she goes through too much when she sees me play. So she cooks or reads. She will run to the screen when she hears that I have scored. For her the most important thing is for me to be happy away from football.

My dad sends me a message after every game. "You were good, I'm proud of you." Or conversely: "I didn't think you were good." At least he tells me what he thinks and feels, not just what I want to hear.

I get along very well with my parents. However, occasionally things arise which can bring about a bit of tension, which happens in all families. Yes, life isn't always rosy. This tension can get to me.

At the end of 2016, I was going through a barren period where I wasn't scoring. I was getting ready for my short Christmas break, the first one with my little daughter. I had planned to go to the United States with Erika. Then we were going to get all the Griezmanns together in the mountains, more specifically in Megève, in the Haute-Savoie. I had intended to rent a lovely little warm chalet where there were things to do each day until December 28th, when I had to start back with Atlético.

But for years my mum had arranged a Christmas meal for all the family as well as close friends. The point of getting together was so we could eat, drink wine, talk, eat again and then return to the table. In short, to pile on the kilos! At the start of December she came to visit us in Madrid. Before I left to meet up with the team for our pre-match preparation, she asked me about the guest list for our wedding. As I know her very well, I replied: "You'll see it when it's ready." But she insisted, wanting to know the identity of the guests, especially if the people she really wanted to see were on it.

I had left home at a very young age. Through the nature of events I have only kept in contact with very few, if any, of her friends or even uncles and cousins. Due to the distance it was impossible to forge links. I told mum this lots of times and I could see she didn't like it.

Then we talked about Christmas. I explained my wonderful plan to her, with stars in my eyes. Maud was there, as was Erika. I was fine, right into my speech, defending my choice of going to the mountains. Except that, for my mum, this wasn't such a great thing. I could only assume that the guest list thing hadn't gone down well. Suddenly I felt uncomfortable. Disappointed that I couldn't generate a reaction from her, I left for the hotel upset, dwelling on this issue.

The next day we were playing Espanyol at the Vicente Calderón. We were on a run of three defeats in five games. We needed a win so as not to be cut adrift. But nobody scored. I did have the chance to do so. It would have done me the world of good to put it away because I hadn't found the net since scoring against Valencia two-and-a-half months previously. In the move, the midfielder Nicolás Gaitán gives me a very good ball. I'm five metres from goal, all alone. But I scuff my shot and the keeper saves it without stretching himself. That's why the mind is so important. If I had already seen the enthusiasm on my mum's face, if she had told me: "There's no worry about the guest list for your wedding," well, maybe I'd have scored. I'm not looking for excuses. That doesn't mean it was because of my mum that I didn't convert against Diego López. On the other hand, I do feel the need to be happy off the pitch in order to be good on it.

Don't worry, in the end these breaks were enjoyable. The simple world of 'holiday' makes me smile and cheer up when I'm not feeling great, when tiredness takes over, especially on the mental side. The stress of travelling, of the matches or of the shoots with sponsors goes away when rest takes effect. I need that to get away from football and to clear my head. Erika, who sees me every day, is the only one who really understands.

I am different on holiday. I want to do things, to walk, go to restaurants, take in shows, visit places, while during the season I never leave my house. There's no dining in town, no trips. I even avoid walking in front of my house, except when I need to take the dog out. I prefer to stay in, recuperate, watch television and make the most of being with my daughter. From time to time, I would like do more but my legs, my body and my head don't want to! Playing every three days is time-consuming. And for home games as well as away ones we go away the night before, which means sleeping in a hotel. Therefore I only have one desire when I'm home: to stay still.

These December holidays took place in the States first of all, and they were only with Erika. Then they were in Megève. A chalet, a chimney, maté, and the whole family: what more could you ask for your daughter's first Christmas? This digression was a return to childhood, with devilish games of Cluedo. No need to tell you who found Doctor Black's killer the most: me of course! On the morning of the 25th we opened the presents. Mia was spoiled, with toys and albums of French songs. Good: at home the music reverberates in Spanish. The next day we hit the heights to see the snow and to do a bit of sledding because I'm aware that my contract forbids me from ski-ing. We also indulged in some zip-lining in the trees, triggering a lot of crazy family laughter. The maté was never far away. I even managed to convert my brother Théo. He served me a few and he makes it very well.

The holidays completed, I immediately switched back into competition mode. There was only one thing I couldn't wait to do: start playing again. And in doing so to score more goals to help the team win. This would require working twice as hard, aware that these are my team-mates in whom I have total confidence, and who will take me to the top.

(1) Parisian district.

10

WAKE-UP CALL

A father's instinct isn't wrong. It is wonderfully sharp. When the daily sports paper *L'Équipe* revealed that five players from the France Under-21 team had sneaked off to Paris after a win against Norway in Le Havre in a Euro 2013 play-off game, publishing the information in the hours which followed our elimination in the return leg near Oslo, the identity of all the 'culprits' hadn't been disclosed. Especially mine. But my dad knew immediately. Or at least he guessed. He knows me, he is hyper-sensitive when it comes to me.

A little perspective is called for in this matter. The consequences were critical: while I was knocking on the door of *Les Bleus*, I was banned from all national teams by the French Federation's disciplinary committee until December 31st, 2013. I was 21. It was a blow right to my heart, I was wounded. But I accepted what happened. It also allowed me to mature, to understand better my duties and the demands of a top level footballer. This is not a stain on my path but an important step on it. I have become more professional since, paying attention to the slightest detail. Yes, since this episode I have become a different person, a different player. Basically, a different man. This was, paradoxically, a blessing in disguise.

Let's rewind the film to Friday, October 12th, 2012, at the Stade Océane in Le Havre, a modern arena of 25,000 capacity, which was inaugurated three months earlier.

To reach the finals of the European Under-21 tournament, which was going to take place in Israel the following June, we only had one last step to negotiate: knock out Norway over two games. The obstacle does not seem insurmountable, especially as our run until then had been exemplary: first place in the group with seven wins and only one defeat. And to think that France, who had been European Champions in this age group in 1998, hadn't figured in the final phase of the tournament since 2006.

Our generation is equipped to do this. In goal there is Ali Ahamada, the defence is made up of the captain, Sebastien Corchia, plus Raphaël Varane, Chris Mavinga and Eliaquim Mangala. In midfield there is Yann M'Vila – who usually plays with the senior team and who already has 22 caps – Rémy Cabella, Vincent Pajot and Clément Grenier, while Wissam Ben Yedder and Anthony Knockaert are in attack. I am not picked from the start, although I usually am. I'm on the bench next to Alexandre Lacazette, Josuha Guilavogui. Benjamin Stambouli and Yacine Brahimi.

The game kicks-off at 6.45pm in light rain. In the 22nd minute Varane, who is already at Real Madrid, meets a Knockaert corner with a header. It will turn out to be the only goal of a game which was interrupted after an hour when six pro-Palestinian protesters, calling for the tournament to be cancelled, invaded the field before being evicted by stewards! Our coach, Erick Mombaerts, waited until the 77th minute before letting me on, replacing Cabella. *Les Bleuets (1)* are in a strong position before the return leg. Even a 2-1 defeat would put us through. The second game comes four days later in Drammen, a town whose population is 65,000, and which lies right at the end of a fjord in the county of Buskerud. The legendary Ole Einar Bjørndalen, who was eight times Olympic champion in the biathlon, hails from there.

If France seem in an ideal position before the return leg, I wasn't happy at the time. I was angry, frustrated at not starting the game. The coach had decided to go with Knockaert, who was playing for Leicester City at the time. He had played well, that wasn't the problem. I was just pissed off about not playing. That's all.

When we were gathered at our hotel on the Saturday night, some of us were in a room where we talked about things after dinner. There was Yann M'Vila, Chris Mavinga, Wissam Ben Yedder and M'Baye Niang. Chris likes to dance, and so to relax and take his mind off things, he put on some music. We were putting the world to rights, speaking about how things were at our clubs or with France Under-21s, about our ambitions.

It was after midnight when one of us received a phone call. A friend told Chris that there was a party going on right now in Paris which quite a few players were attending. We all looked at each other. "So what do we do? Are we going or not?" The desire was there. But the questions came thick and fast. "*It would be cool to go but we're a long way away*", "*How would we get there?*", "*What if the coach finds out?*" We eventually decided to do this Parisian road trip, hoping we wouldn't be caught by the staff.

So, the day after our win against Norway, the five of us got into a car as quietly as possible and headed to the capital, which was 180 kilometres from Le Havre. A friend of one of the players, who had attended the game, was at the wheel. The atmosphere was pretty chipper on the whole of the trip. The car reverberated with our songs and those on the radio. The kilometres were quickly devoured.

It was very late when we arrived at the party, which took place at the Crystal Lounge, a trendy nightclub a stone's throw from the Champs-Élysées. We were barely there for an hour. Then we left at dawn on Sunday, asking the driver to get us back to Le Havre as quickly as possible so that we could sleep for a few hours – and most of all avoid getting a roasting.

When I got to my room the pressure was off. I was settled. But I felt that I had just made a big mistake. Yeah, I had screwed up.

Up till then, nobody knew about it. Neither the coaches, nor the general public. It had been a very short night. We had a morning session at Le Havre's training ground and then we flew off to Norway in the afternoon, 48 hours before the second leg. I don't know how the rumour started, but it was already doing the rounds on the plane. The whisper was that some players had gone out the night before. No names were mentioned. Once we got to our hotel in Drammen, the captain, Sébastien Corchia and vice-captain, Raphaël Varane, hinted that they knew that Yann M'Vila and M'Baye Niang were among the players concerned and that there were three others.

Chris Mavinga went to find the coach, Erick Mombaerts, to tell him that he had been involved. Through the captains, the coach made it known that he wanted the two others to come forward, and he conducted his own investigation, contacting the night clerk at the Hôtel Mercure in Le Havre. Then he and his staff learned that Wissam Ben Yedder had also been there. I was the only one missing… To be honest, I waited to see if it would blow over. Of course, if the coach had come to ask me if I had been there, I wouldn't have lied. But I didn't want to turn myself in and I doubted the others would give up my name.

Finally, a few hours later, Mombaerts asked me to join him in the hotel lounge. "Were you with the others?" he asked. Either someone had tipped him off or he was bluffing. I didn't shy away and I told the truth. "Yes, I was there." He expressed his deep disappointment, stating that he didn't think I was the kind of person who would make such a mistake. He was with his assistant, Patrick Gonfalone, who has a loud voice. "Yes, I know I screwed up," I added. "I was angry and I behaved like a spoiled, sulking child. I'm sorry…" There is no doubt I had broken the rules and made one hell of a mistake, but there was no need to keep going on about it. In any case, even though he had identified us all, he decided not to punish us, at least not before the decisive game. Qualifying for the Euro Under-21s was the priority.

Concentration had to be at a maximum. But our match in Norway turned into a nightmare. It was almost the same team which had started the first leg. The only changes: Joshua Guilavogui and Alexandre Lacazette were in from the start.

As for me, I stayed confined to the bench, while Wissam Ben Yedder was in the stands. *Les Bleuets* shipped water very quickly. Chris Mavinga soon picked up a yellow card, making two mistakes which resulted in as many goals. We were 3-0 down after 27 minutes! Although Guilavogui gave us hope of a miracle just before half-time, Yann M'Vila just wasn't with it. He lost possession, which Norway capitalised on, and they added a fifth goal when the goalkeeper made an error in coming for the ball. On the hour mark the coach brought on Henri Saivet and M'Baye Niang. But the conditions weren't helping us: an artificial pitch with a greasy surface which was drenched with water as a result of the non-stop rain which had fallen since the start of the afternoon.

I entered the fray in the 64th minute, replacing Guilavogui. Twenty minutes later Alex Lacazette reduced the arrears and then got himself sent off. Then it was my turn, in the 87th minute, to renew hope by scoring with an angled shot. Just one more goal and we'd qualify. We laid siege to the opposing goal. We pushed and we pushed. But there would be no further score. The referee blew for the end of the game. Norway had won 5-3, thereby booking their ticket to Israel.

The disappointment was immense. So was the sadness. Ours was a talented generation but it missed the boat. No excuse. I knew then that it was all going to kick off, that our jaunt from Le Havre was going to leak out. The press began to be pushy, trying to gather as much information about those who had gone out. They needed people to blame. At that time the France team was wracked with doubts and the subject of controversy. Two years earlier, in 2010, in Knysna, in South Africa, there had been the strike at training when the players were entrenched in the bus, all of which contributed to the first round elimination in the World Cup.

Then, in 2012, there was also the Euros in Poland and Ukraine. Laurent Blanc's *Bleus* lost in the quarter-final to Spain, the eventual winners. But the public had mostly remembered

Sami Nasri's gesture of putting his index finger over his mouth as if to say to his detractors, including the press and certain individual critics in the dressing room, to shut up following his goal against England. Basically, we had to be irreproachable and we weren't. Neither from a sporting point of view, nor a moral one.

In my heart, I thought: "We're going down." It's clear that if we had beaten Norway, as we should have done, this business would not have had the same exposure. The whole thing may never have come out. But the fact remains our names were splashed on the front page.

My father had guessed before mine had appeared. I felt guilty. I hadn't taken into account the warnings I had been given, notably from Éric Olhats. I hadn't appreciated enough what my status as a professional footballer and Under-21 international represented. I hadn't really been aware of the fact that I had become a public figure, and as such I couldn't simply behave the way I wanted. I had responsibilities, both for my club and for the national team, where I represent my country. Yes, I got slapped. And it was a big slap. The best of my life! It was beneficial. It did me good.

Éric wasn't pleased and neither were my parents. I felt a lot of anger inside. I knew I'd hurt my family. I had to change all this. Both my dad, who coached young footballers, and my mum yelled at me. I could tell they were annoyed. Éric and my dad got me to re-focus by holding an improvised 'crisis meeting' at my place in San Sebastián, where they reminded me of the importance of a footballer's image and that in no way should the Griezmann name be tarnished. Then, after a few days, they got behind me and helped me get back on my feet because I was so upset. My sister and brother were also supportive. This protective environment allowed me to forget about things and to bounce back, and to concentrate solely on football.

Unlike the other culprits, apart from M'Baye Niang, who had just joined AC Milan, I wasn't playing in France. Real Sociedad pampered me upon my return to Spain. They really helped me through this difficult period. The coach, Philippe Montanier, even tried to joke around, to make me smile again, because I was so caught up in myself. The team captain came out with some encouraging words, assuring me: "You don't need to worry here. We'll look after you." He also told the press: "We need Antoine." My team-mates pushed me on, and I became as motivated as possible, more determined and with the desire to surpass myself. I doubled my efforts in training.

The criticism, quite naturally, did not do us any favours. The defender Sébastien Corchia had some harsh things to say. After the elimination by Norway he battered us in the papers and on the radio. That hurt me. After all, he was our captain. Of course, we had messed up. But we didn't need the person with the armband to hammer us publicly. However, I did appreciate Raphaël Varane's response. Instead of pointing the finger at us, he adopted the right tone on the issue: "Yes, they did something stupid. They know it. But you have to forgive."

But I wasn't out of the woods. On October 18th, two days after the game in Drammen, the French Federation's disciplinary commission got together. We were going to be summoned and, as the press release had indicated, "answer for our actions" in relation to our evening outing when we had joined up with *Les Bleuets*. The press had a field day. Yann M'Vila was even more in the eye of the storm because he had been 'called to order' by the same commission for refusing to shake the hand of the coach and the player who was coming on for him when he was replaced in the quarter-final of the Euros with the senior side. I was lucky to be living in Spain and having less exposure.

It was one morning at the beginning of November when we went before the committee at the French Football Federation headquarters in the Boulevard de Grenelle in Paris' 15th arrondissement. Yann, Chris, M'Baye, Wissam and I were all there. So was Erick Mombaerts. He was no longer in charge of France Under-21s, having resigned in the wake of our pitiful elimination. Opposite us were the Federation's top brass. We were accompanied by a club representative or an agent in some cases. As a way of proving that Real Sociedad were with me in this hearing and they were showing solidarity, the vice-president himself made the journey to Paris. Each of us spoke in turn. The hearing was like a court case. We were standing in front of a big table where, around the sides, the federal executives were sitting. When it was my turn to explain and defend myself, I turned to the coach, "I know we screwed up. I'm really sorry, but that's how it is…" I didn't know what to add. It was too late for regrets. The best thing to do was be quiet and accept the disciplinary measure.

Erick Mombaerts' assistant judged us very harshly, as if we were a bunch of little pricks, suggesting that it was because of us that the coach had lost his job. We deserved that, even though it was difficult to hear and to accept. Obviously I am sad for Mombaerts, but it is only because of us that France were knocked out? I don't know. We had begun the game in Norway very badly, and we were walked all over by a disciplined and well-organised team. We conceded two goals which were avoidable and mentally we lost it, reacting far too late. Once again, I accept our mistakes.

In fact, while some of the players appealed their penalty, I did not. My reasoning was thus: 'You shut your mouth and keep a low profile. You'll see out your ban and then that will be that.' The sentence was severe. Perhaps, in light of what had happened in Knysna and in Euro 2012, the FFF *(2)* wanted to make an example of us. The message was clear: zero tolerance. No favours, we'll bring the players into line! With the election for a new president just one month away, the institution needed to re-affirm its authority.

The disciplinary commission's verdict was most extreme in Yann M'Vila's case, banning him until June 30th, 2014, meaning he could kiss goodbye to the World Cup in Brazil. At 22 he was barely older than us, but he was certainly more experienced, and he was considered to be behind the trip. It's true that he had been made available for the Under-21s to supervise us and guide us towards qualification. But, I insist, we were all responsible, Yann no more than the rest of us. There was no leader and no followers. We share the blame. Nobody was under any influence. If, for example, Yann hadn't gone to Paris, then the other four still would have. We wanted to have some fun. We were going out of our minds! We needed to get away, and we did it at the worst possible time.

For Chris, M'Baye, Wissam and me, the punishment is the same: 'suspended from all national teams from Monday November 12th 2012 to Tuesday December 31st 2013' according to the press release. We never saw each other again. We are still mates, even though we did something daft.

Sébastien Corchia, who was playing for Lille at the time, was called up to the senior side for the first time in August 2016. He played his first minutes for *Les Bleus* the following November, in a friendly. We have never spoken about what happened. I am not a vindictive person even though, when he turned up at Clairefontaine with the senior side it got to me a bit. I was a bit distant initially, but things got forgotten very quickly. This sanction could have been a killer. But I knew how to turn it into something positive. I gave everything I had for Real Sociedad and I changed my behaviour. The reward came when I was approaching the end of my 'punishment'. Didier Deschamps telephoned me to tell me that he had been following my performances and that I might have my chance. That was a real boost.

When I was banned from the national teams for 13 months, I found the penalty severe, a little excessive. Today, as an important player in the France team, I understand better. And if a team-mate was to make the same kind of mistake as we did, sneaking out of a team gathering to secretly go on a night out, I would ask for an example to be made of him, too. When you're with the senior team, and as soon as you wear the blue shirt, you can't afford to have the slightest indiscretion off the field.

(1) Nickname of the French Under-21 team

(2) Fédération Française de Football.

11

MATÉ CULTURE

Rubbing shoulders with Uruguayan and Argentinian team-mates at Real Sociedad and Atlético Madrid makes an impression on you. I feel good being in their company. I like these people, their way of life, how they are positive in all circumstances, their big-heartedness, their state of mind and their solidarity. They are the kind who will do anything for you in order to make you happy and never complain while, in their country, people aren't rolling in money. I live like a South American. I often share a maté in the dressing room before training, with music in the background. And we talk, about anything and everything, in good humour and simplicity. It's a real moment of conviviality between friends.

I'm addicted to maté. It's the traditional South American drink, which comes from the Guarani people. There is caffeine and stimulating properties in this infusion of yerba maté leaves. And, besides, it's good for your health. It's drunk from a calabash, a gourd, with the aid of a bombilla, a kind of metal straw through which you suck.

It's thanks to Carlos Bueno that I discovered this beverage which contains vitamins and minerals. It began with him. He used to drink lots of it. I was on my own in San Sebastián, so much so that I followed him everywhere. Often I would even sleep at his place. I didn't have a driving licence, so we would go to training together. I used to watch him prepare his maté. I used to drink it in front of the TV when he was taking a siesta.

At first I didn't like it at all. I needed time to get used to its sensations. It's a hot, bitter drink which doesn't really have much taste. I was just happy enough to do what he did before I really got into it. Today I can't do without maté. It gives me a boost, like coffee. I've got all the equipment at home, the Uruguay captain, Diego Godín, who has represented his country more than 100 times, gave me the complete package.

Often it is me who brings the maté to training. It also comes with me when I'm on away trips and at Clairefontaine. Even on a photoshoot, when it drags on and on, I find it relaxing to wet my lips in the calabash which has my name on. I have become a specialist, even better than Godín! You have to be careful not to drown it, like with pastis, and not to burn the grass at the bottom. Everyone has their own technique and it's not easy. Maté is also beneficial because it cleanses your body and helps you hydrate better. I'm able to have some before a match. I also drink it in Mâcon. My brother has got into it, and Erika also drinks it except when it is too hot. It's even better when it's cold outside because it's a very hot drink. I either buy packets of them in a supermarket or I ask Nico Gaitán and Godín, who have their own places where they get it. Careful now, it is not a drug. I have two or three a day and when I go without it I'm fine.

I owe Carlos Bueno a lot, and not just for the maté. He only stayed one season at Real Sociedad, having come on loan one summer from Penarol in Uruguay, which is his homeland. Beforehand he had played for Paris Saint-Germain, where he won the French Cup in 2006. He scored 12 goals in the Basque Country and helped us become second division champions. Because he's eleven years older than me, I used to call Carlos 'Papi' *(1)*. I was 18 and he was kind of a dad to me. He took me under his wing and gave me loads of advice. I watched him a lot, observing the way he played with his back to goal and the quality of his heading game even though he was only 1.78 metres (5'8") tall.

Carlos is the most significant team-mate I have had, the one who helped me the most, both on and off the field. I learned lots from him and he made me a better player in front of goal, smarter and more opportunistic. I liked how he moved in attack. We were very complementary all season. He made goals for me and I for him. We were always looking for each other on the field. He was more of a killer than me in the box, less technical but he had a will of iron with his sliding tackles and wasn't shy when it came to getting stuck in.

I nicked his heading game and I'm proud of the result. Every time the ball hit his head it was a goal. I took inspiration from this and I perfected it. Today I love to use my head. The sense of timing in order to make better contact with the ball doesn't necessarily come from him because I could already jump pretty well. He was more valuable to me in the art of finishing, with how he moved around the danger zone. He showed me how to do it. I analysed his game and how he would attack the ball. I began to reproduce what he did in games of head-tennis and then in match situations. He still hasn't hung up his boots at 38 years of age.

My South American passion also includes a pronounced taste for barbecues. The Argentinians probably have the best meat in the world and the *asado* technique – grilling – is a way of life. I'm not bad at that lark. At my house I have had a specific area assigned for barbecuing.

I love having friends round. Diego Godín has us round at his place, too. He is the boss in that field. I invited him to ours because I know he likes to do the preparation; I make the most of it by watching him as closely as possible so I can see how he places the meat perfectly flat, leaving the fire on one side. I enjoy the relaxed atmosphere at these times: you watch your meat cook, you talk, you discuss things standing up with a glass in your hand. The women are there, and small groups begin to form. Nobody has their phone. These are timeless, special moments.

I have had a Uruguayan team-mate ever since I began playing with the pros. I feel good in their company. They are always smiling, creating a good mood. I love Uruguay, though I have generally chosen the United States for my holidays, especially to attend NBA games.

I had a small basketball court built in front of the house in Madrid. Sometimes I train there to unwind. I also play basketball on the Xbox. Most of the time, whether I'm on the console or playing outside at home, I'm the Chicago Bears.

I came to basketball late. It was Carlos Vela, who signed for Real Sociedad in the summer of 2011, who got me into it. When I arrived for training he would often be talking abut the NBA, the American championship, with Gorka Elustondo. I had a few things in common with the pair of them.

I began to take an interest in it so I could join in their conversation. I didn't know much and I didn't have any kind of basketball culture. At home I started to look at videos on YouTube. I analysed how quite a few people played and then I came across Derrick Rose. It was like love at first sight. I combed through all of his performances which were available. I must have watched dozens of them in just one afternoon.

In December 2015, during the holidays, I even went to Chicago specially to see him! I had been able to attend a Bulls training session, thanks to the power forward Nikola Mirotić. A Montenegrin by birth, he stood 2.08 metres (6'8") tall and was declared a Spanish citizen in 2011. He played four seasons for Real Madrid, which is where I got to know him. I was even able to try out a few shoots on the court. But, unfortunately for me, Derrick Rose had already left. I was disappointed. So it was like a dream to see him for the first time in a match, even more so because it was in the legendary United Center, where Michael Jordan slammed in so many dunks and became NBA champion. With Rose so close to me I said to myself: "At last I can see you!" I had gone to Illinois with my brother and my sister. We could have called this trip 'Siblings in Chicago.' The Bulls lost against the Brooklyn Nets. It seems Maud and Théo jinxed it!

I also took in some NBA games two years ago, this time in the play-offs. I went with Maud to Houston to see James Harden's Rockets, and then to San Francisco to watch Stephen Curry's Golden State Warriors. I loved the atmosphere.

What's more, pretty much everyone wears the same shirt in the play-offs. In Houston it was red. When the camera spots someone who isn't wearing it, the picture is beamed on the giant screen and they're booed by the fans. It's the same in San Francisco, where the shirts are yellow. There's a tremendous atmosphere in both these halls, steeped in good spirit. It's a full-on show. I like this mentality. It's a shame we footballers don't have it.

For example, I think it would be great to see the whole stadium decked out in blue when France play at home. The NBA should be a source of inspiration. For me, there's another example to consider: respect for the referee. Over there, if you dispute or mouth off or even if you speak to the referee you have a free shot awarded against you. This could be applied in Spain, for example, by being penalised with a free-kick in the final 30 or 40 metres. I'm convinced this would bring about fewer arguments with referees.

I feel good in the United States. Every house has its American flag as a means of displaying and asserting its patriotic pride. I like the way Americans view things, and also this mixture with Blacks, Chinese, Latinos etc… One day I could easily play in the States. If possible in a club which owns a franchise: that would be ideal.

There's no hurry. I still have time on my side so I'm not going to go rushing into things. But I would like to get to know such an experience, to live the American way and soak up that culture. I can mainly envisage doing it towards the end of my career, like Thierry Henry. The Spanish World Cup winner, David Villa, played for New York City. I spoke about it with him. He thrived over there and his family was more than happy.

Getting back to South America, I also like the zeal and the passion which the Uruguayans have, and also their simplicity. Diego Godín has spoken to me about hunting wild boar with his dad. They leave together for the whole day, with some maté in their Thermos flask. In the evening they return home with the game and put it on the barbecue. That's tempting…

I have the Uruguayan flag as part of my WhatsApp profile and I know the chants of the Penarol fans because Carlos Bueno played there. I learned the songs on YouTube. The Uruguay link was there again with Martin Lasarte, the Real Sociedad coach who handed me my debut. He, too, gave me useful advice and not just relating to football. He was so generous. He was without his family, who had stayed back home, but he often invited me round to share a plate of pasta. He would show me Copa Libertadores games so I could appreciate the incredible commitment which the players had and the ferocity of the challenges. They were aggressive, as we are at Atlético, where you run, attack and defend like crazy. The intensity is total.

Gonzalo Castro, whom we all call 'Chori', was a team-mate for whom I have great affection. A three-times champion of Uruguay with Nacional Montevideo, he joined Málaga and now plays for Club Nacional de Football. Like his compatriots he was older than me but he remained young in his head. He would rib people but at the same time he'd be working for the team. His joie de vivre at Real Sociedad was permanent. That's also why I get on so well with Paul Pogba: we are always having a laugh together.

The Uruguay team, *La Celeste (2)* as they are known, have one of my favourite strikers in their ranks: Edinson Cavani. I was applauding him long before he shone at PSG. He is a real number nine, a killer in front of goal, who also loves to defend and press. The way he calls for the ball is outstanding. He always seems to be well-placed, even though he doesn't always hit the target. It's impressive the number of chances he makes for himself. That's the most important thing in football.

When I watch him play I pay close attention so I can learn.

I am inspired by him. In addition I like his personality. I don't know him but, via Twitter, he has invited me to have a maté with him. As with all Uruguayans he has an exemplary mentality. He works for the team and the smile doesn't leave his face. He plays up front in the national team with Luis Suarez. He isn't as hot-blooded as the Barça striker, who as we know bit one of the Italian defenders in the World Cup!

Although I have la grinta *(3)* I rarely lose my temper on the field. I have only received one red card, and rarely pick up yellows. I can get annoyed – for example when I'm flagged offside by the referee's assistant even though I know for sure I'm not – but you can count the number of times that's happened on the fingers of one hand.

Anyway, the more there is at stake, the calmer I am. Sometimes an opposing defender will try to wind me up and provoke me. But he gets discouraged when he sees I don't rise to the bait ... Okay, I moan a bit. I don't like losing, which is the same for any top-level sportsman. Nor do I accept a lack of desire or not giving one's all on the field.

One pre-season with Atlético, there was an instance when I had to put a young player right during training. He had just got into the first team and he thought he had done the hard bit. I made it clear to him that he was wrong. Seeing him behave like an amateur while I, who had less to prove, was giving everything, infuriated me. Yes, I can get a bit hot-blooded! I have had aggression ever since I was very young. Like a real South American...

(1) Grandad
(2) Sky Blues
(3) Tenacity

12

BLUE IS THE COLOUR

The tears of disenchantment took time to dry. Spontaneously, these drops of salty water beaded up on my devastated face. They demonstrated my dismay and emotion while removing the stress. The loud applause of the 74,000 spectators in Rio de Janeiro's legendary Maracana Stadium wasn't enough to comfort me. Far from it.

On this Friday, July 4th 2014, France were knocked out of the World Cup quarter-finals by Germany. The dream of being crowned kings of the planet in the country of football was yanked away from us, smashed by the clinical realism of Die Mannshaft (1).

The nerves gave way to despair. The frustration was such that the only thing I could do was burst into tears when, after five minutes of stoppage time, the Argentinian referee, Nestor Pitana, blew to signal the end of the fantastic journey.

The tears bring some relief, but as well as being a promise of the future, they say all kinds of things. When I was wandering in the middle of the pitch like a lost soul after the fatal verdict, Rio Mavuba attempted to comfort me. Other team-mates tried in turn but the disappointment was so strong that it was natural for me just to cry in their arms. It was impossible to stem these tears, which were my way of illustrating the cruelty of this outcome. I was wrecked. It had killed us all.

In the dressing room, while our eyes were fixed on the floor, the coach began to speak. Since the start of the tournament his speeches were usually punctuated with applause. Not this time. It's all gone down the pan, which is basically the feeling we expressed after Didier Deschamps' words: "We're good here. We're not going back. Brazil is our home. This is our home…" We didn't want to turn back. We were so good here in this cocoon. It was horrible.

Later that evening I summed up my feelings in a tweet: 'Great sadness, but proud of our World Cup…We'll come back even stronger,' alluding to Euro 2016. Through the photos and videos we received I am aware of how excited the French people were and that the euphoria was increasing. From thousands of kilometres away, it was the chance to think of all the people in the streets who were watching the games on giant screens and expressing their joy.

We had fulfilled our objective by reaching the quarter-finals, but I was hoping for even more. We were keen to keep the enjoyment going. It was cruel. We created lots of chances in this game and overall we didn't deserve to lose. This World Cup would end with the unpleasant feeling that we could have achieved more. We had been at our base camp at Ribeirão Preto, in São Paulo state, since the June 9th, where we were spoiled by the hotel staff. It would be heartbreaking to leave…

I love the blue shirt and the values it represents. Nineteen days from my 19th birthday I first had the opportunity to sport international colours. I was playing for Real Sociedad in the second division at the time. As a starter in the first team, I was beginning to score goals regularly.

On March 2nd, 2010, in Saint-Jean-de-Braye, in the Loiret region, the France Under-19s coach, Francis Smerecki, picked me to start a friendly against Ukraine. We played at the Sports Complex of Petit Bois – you don't forget that – and the admission was free.

We had quite an attacking line-up because, up front, I was alongside Yannis Tafer, not far from our captain, Gilles Sunu. Despite everything, this friendly finished goalless. Along with the goalkeeper, Abdoulaye Diallo, I was the only new player in the team, but I played the whole game. Two days later, against the same opposition, again in the Loiret – although this time at Saint-Denis-de-l'Hôtel – we won 2-1. I started this match on the bench, from where I emerged in the 69th minute to replace Alexandre Lacazette, who had opened the scoring. Nineteen minutes later, I hit the winner for *Les Bluets* with a shot from the middle of the goal.

It was the ideal preparation for the Under-19 Championships, which France were organising in Basse-Normandie. I went on to play in all our five matches. I had no joy in our opening fixture against Holland (4-1), but I bagged a brace against Austria (5-0). As a substitute for our final group game against England (1-1), I came on for the last quarter of an hour. I didn't miss a minute of our semi-final against Croatia (2-1) and I was again a starter for the final against Spain in Caen's Michel d'Ornano Stadium on July 30th.

We claimed the title in front of over 20,000 spectators with a 2-1 victory, thanks to goals from Gilles Sunu and Alexandre Lacazette. There was joy, of course, but it was tainted with a slight bitterness because I sprained my ankle with my first touch of the ball. It swelled up and the coach, cautiously, withdrew me at half-time. I managed to be fit enough to help Gueïda Fofana *(2)* and his armband lift the trophy.

This generation of players born in 1991 looked great. It was strong, with Loïc Négo and Timothée Kolodziejczak in defence, Francis Coquelin and Fofana in the midfield and Lacazette and Cédric Bakambu up front. But the one who stood out for me the most was Gaël Kakuta, an attacking midfielder who was two centimetres (over half an inch) shorter than me.

He had been at Chelsea since the age of 16 after moving from Lens. He made his Premier League bow in November 2009 when he came on for Nicolas Anelka against Wolves. His coach, the Italian Carlo Ancelotti, admitted afterwards: "He has so much ability and he has an excellent character. I have never seen a player of that age with such talent. He is not very strong physically but, technically, he is ready." It was a view I shared. I have rarely seen a player as good, someone who can make such a difference by accelerating, just in one movement. He is currently playing for Rayo Vallecano, where he was on loan during 2014/2015. He has also played for Fulham, Bolton Wanderers, Dijon, Vitesse Arnhem, Lazio, Sevilla, Hebei China Fortune, Deportivo La Coruña and Amiens! It's such a shame he hasn't achieved the success he deserves at the numerous clubs he's been at. I was fortunate to blossom at Real Sociedad. He hasn't experienced such happiness.

Gaël is different to other players. He was one of the leaders of the France Under-20 team which took part in the World Cup for that age group in Colombia in the summer of 2011. We were heavily beaten by the host country in our opening game in

Bogotá on July 30th. We lost 4-1 in front of 42,000 spectators, and one of their goals was scored by James Rodriguez, who would be signed by Real Madrid for 80 million euros after a stunning 2014 World Cup where he scored six goals.

Three days later, again in Bogotá, we saw off South Korea 3-1. As had been the case in the previous game, I played 83 minutes. We then beat Mali 2-0 in Cali on August 5th to book our ticket into the round of 16. I came off after an hour, still not having scored. But there was no reason for my morale to be affected.

The atmosphere in the squad was excellent. Practically all of us knew each other and our victory in the European Under-19 Championship the previous year had strengthened our bond. We would often burst out laughing because we shared the same kind of lunacy. However, that doesn't mean that there was no discipline. With the coach, Francis Smerecki, who had joined the national coaching set-up (DTN) in 2004, we walked a straight line, a bit like in the army.

We had arrived in Colombia a few days before the World Cup had kicked-off, and I was sharing my room with Lacazette. One evening we were invited into Kakuta and Négo's. There was a lot of chatter and a lot of laughter. It's just that the coach's room was next door and the noise we were making echoed around the floor. Smerecki began to lose his patience and so he got up and knocked on the door. Alex went to open it while Gaël leapt up in a reflex action and then dived down to hide under the bed. "Right, get out of the room," Smerecki said. It was past midnight. The staff woke up the whole team to ask him to get out. The players, some of them woken from their sleep, did what they were told. We all stood outside our doors in the long hotel corridor. The coach began to speak in a military tone: "Now everyone go back to their room. We've got an important competition to prepare for. Go back to bed and, I repeat, you are no longer allowed to go in other people's rooms." To be honest we didn't always respect this instruction…

We knocked out Ecuadaor in Cartagena, in the round of 16. In the 75th minute, after Fofana had created the opening, I deflected the ball from the left to the far post, where it took me two attempts to score from close range. It was the only goal of the game. I came off a minute later. In the quarter-final in Cali it was Nigeria who gave way, 3-2, during extra-time. The Under-20s World Cup has been around since 1977 but this was the first time that France had reached the last four. Unfortunately Portugal did for us in the semi-finals. In the searing heat of Medellin, in front of more than 40,000 people, we lost 2-0 on August 17th, 2011. As in the previous round I played the whole game. It was a tense, scrappy encounter with seven yellow cards. Even though Lacazette opened the scoring in the match for third place against Mexico in Bogotá, we lost 3-1 and ended up fourth.

Alex won the Bronze Boot for his five goals in the tournament. I loved playing with him. We would try to find each other all the time in training and in games. No doubt a bit too much. Once, right in the middle of a session, Gilles Sunu snapped and said, "Hey! You're pissing everyone off playing with each other all the time! Pass to other people." Seeing this big fella get mad and sulk made us laugh, even if he was right. Other team-mates thought like him and there was the danger they would take umbrage at our collusion.

I only have good memories of the Under-20s. We left nothing to chance, especially when it came to the preparation.

So that we could get used to the altitude, the sleep and the food in Colombia, we played a few friendlies in Peru, straight after an intense July training camp in Tignes, at the foot of the mountains. At an altitude of 2,100 metres we sweated on the pitches in Savoie, but also on the bike rides and the runs around the lake.

I was back on the France Under-21 train, so to speak, at the end of this saga. I had first boarded it in November 2010 for a friendly against Russia in Le Mans. I had been called up by Erick Mombaerts, who had been in charge since 2008 following the departure of René Girard. I didn't know many people but it was a chance to take stock of things. I had been sent on in the 62nd minute, at the same time as Emmanuel Rivière and Eliaquim Mangala. In what was a large review of the squad, where Moussa Sissoko was captain, we lost 1-0. I was called up again three months later, again for a friendly, against Spain in Reims. I started that game which we won 3-2. I returned to the Under-21s in Clermont-Ferrand in October, after the Colombia World Cup. I came on for Gaël Kakuta 20 minutes from the end of a win against Kazakhstan which was vital for our qualification for the European Championships. I hadn't cemented my place but I did my best, for example by scoring and providing an assist in Astana over in Kazakhstan.

Before we were able to qualify for the Euros in Israel, in the summer of 2013, we had to try and trip Norway up again in the play-offs. Our opponents seemed beatable. I didn't start either of the matches, not the first leg in Le Havre, where Raphaël Varane scored the only goal, nor the return four days later in Drammen.

Our elimination in October 2012 had left its mark, and the consequences of our night-time outing between both legs was one of the turning points of my professional life. As you've read, I was suspended from all levels of international football until December 31st, 2013.

The punishement was all the more severe since I was getting nearer the top, the be-all and end-all: the senior side. When I was with the Under-21s I had noticed the facilities at the national football centre at Clairefontaine, with the château and its infrastructures. My aim was to become part of *Les Bleus*. Coming out of a training session, I went to spy on them on the Michel Platini field, which is where they train. Laurent Blanc was coach at the time, and I knew he had been keeping an eye on me because he had already named me in an initial list of 50. I watched Karim Benzema work in front of goal. He hit the net with every shot. I was impressed. 'Ah, yes,' I thought. 'I've still got to keep working. I'm way short of the mark and their level.'

During my suspension I worked hard with Real Sociedad. I had the World Cup in Brazil in the corner of my mind. I didn't really think it would happen, but still. Didier Deschamps' *Bleus* had booked their ticket by overcoming Ukraine, overturning a first leg deficit in the return game at the Stade de France. The following match, the first in 2014, saw Holland pitch up in the Saint-Denis arena for a friendly. There was a chance I would be called up. The media were talking about me, I was scoring more and more in La Liga – I was third top scorer with 15 goals behind Diego Costa and Cristiano Ronaldo – and I had experienced the Champions League. Éric Olhats had suggested to me that I might be in.

A few days before the squad was revealed he asked me to monitor my phone, stating that Didier Deschamps, whom he knows well, had asked for my number. I kept checking all day long. Then he called. I was in the car, so I pulled over onto the side of the road and put on my hazard lights. I needed quiet for such a conversation. The coach had heartening words and confirmed that he was monitoring me. I was touched. Even though he hadn't made me any promises I was like a nutter. I told my parents and my mates. That weekend, boosted by his call, I was even more determined to shine.

My club received the official call-up and passed it on to Éric, telling him not to inform me because they didn't want me to be distracted. Of course he warned me. Things were beginning to get real. But that wasn't enough: I still needed to see my name on the screen.

On February 27th 2014, the day the squad was officially announced, I got home quickly from training. Stuck on my sofa at lunchtime, I saw Didier Deschamps at the FFF's headquarters in Paris start to list the names of the players chosen for the Holland game on March 5th by position and in alphabetical order. For the strikers he began with Karim Benzema and Olivier Giroud. Classic. In theory I should be next. I was, ahead of Dimitri Payet, Loïc Rémy, Franck Ribéry and Mathieu Valbuena. "He is very effective with his club, he scores lot of goals and he makes them," is what the coach said when justifying my inclusion in the 22 names. "He can play in several positions in attack, he's comfortable down the middle or out wide. He is technically very good."

I shouted when my name appeared on the television. I shouted very loudly. I immediately called my parents. My mum was on the other end and I was so happy I was just babbling: I didn't know what to say. I was crying, but crying with joy. I was unable say a word. None would come out of my mouth. I was overcome with emotion. "At last I've made it," best summarises how I was feeling. I had been messed about and suffered from comments made about me, in Mâcon and elsewhere. My parents had heard certain things and I had read things I didn't like, comments on the Internet about how I only thought about going out and that I didn't deserve *Les Bleus*. This first call-up would turn out to be a reward. But it was certainly not an end in itself. No way was I letting go. This was just the start. The hardest part was about to begin. I intended to cling on to this like a dog with a bone so I could jump on the bandwagon and never be left out of the France team.

I was in a room with the other new call-up, Lucas Digne, at Clairefontaine, each with our own little bed. I was fairly relaxed as I held my first press conference on the rostrum. I was cool. I was just thinking about not making too many mistakes in French, since I spoke more often in Spanish, the language in which my conversation is more fluid and natural. I answered spontaneously. The press officer, Philippe Tournon, hadn't needed to brief me: there were no trick questions. I remembered how happy I was to be here, swearing that I was not putting any pressure on myself, that the suspension had done me good and that I had become a different person.

Regarding my position, which was generally down the left at Real, it was pointed out to me that that was Franck Ribéry's position in the national team. I replied that I had no problem playing wherever the coach intended, even in goal if that's what he wanted. I added that for my club I would often play on the right and in the middle, that I was a team player who would put the team first, and that I was someone who wouldn't think twice about passing rather than trying to score at all costs.

In the first training session, I found myself alongside players whom I would normally watch on TV: Ribéry, Hugo Lloris, Karim Benzema, Patrice Evra. It was impressive, and all very new to me. I didn't laugh as I normally do. I was focused in the extreme, anxious to do well and to adapt.

The coaching was top level. Everything was quicker. I liked that. I was giving my all, but feeling a little tense, too. I made sure I didn't make any kind of blunder, being careful of what I said, including in the dressing room. I was made to feel welcome. There was a lot of ribbing going on. I laughed at the leaders' jokes but I didn't make any back. I still felt intimidated.

I had another test to overcome before the Holland game. For me this test was harder and more daunting than playing in front of 50,000 people: sing part of a song, while standing on a chair during our first dinner together, as is the tradition for all new players in the French team.

This good-natured initiation ceremony, where my team-mates would twirl their white serviettes at the end, scared me. Even singing just a handful of words is not something I enjoy doing. Far from it. But you can't get out of it.

I had chosen 'La Bamba,' telling myself that no-one would know if I stumbled on or forgot one of the words. I later found out that Edinson Cavani, whose style of play I appreciate, had also chosen this song when he signed for Paris Saint-Germain.

I wasn't very comfortable at the table. Singing in front of Evra, Ribéry and Benzema: I knew I was going to get a hard time. I was sitting between Hugo Lloris and Raphaël Varane and when it was time for dessert, spoons began to be tapped against the glasses; the signal that the new boys were on. Beads of sweat ran down my face.

I didn't let Lucas Digne kick things off. I wanted to get it over with as quickly as possible. I could feel myself blushing. I stood up on the chair, held a bottle to my mouth as a microphone, and I went for it.

> *Para bailar la bamba se necesita / Una poca de gracia y otra cosita / Ay arriba y arriba, Y arriba y arriba, arriba iré / Yo no soy marinero por tí seré / Para subir al cielo se necesita / Una escalera grande y otra chiquita / Yo no soy marinero, soy capitán...*

These 30 seconds or so felt like an eternity. To help me, the coaching and medical staff joined in with me a bit at the end. Then the applause rang out. Phew! When you really mess things up you can be whistled at and have the serviettes thrown on the ground. Suddenly the pressure was off. I felt good in my bed that evening. I felt calm. Everything became more cool after that.

This ritual, which seems harmless, is something that really matters because it marks the start of an international career. In the light of my own experience I can now have a go at the new guys, staring at the ones who have to do it during dinner so I can make them uncomfortable. It's my way of avenging what I had to go through. These friendly moments, where you are the centre of all attention, take place in good humour. It's only one bad thing you have to go through! Some people just freeze. But, once again, you can't get out of it. Even the coach reminds you of your obligations, telling you privately: "Tonight you are going to sing. So you need to be well prepared..."

Other players have amazing ability in this field. Ousmane Dembélé, for example. He was only 19 when he was called up at the end of August 2016 for the World Cup qualifiers in Italy and Belarus. For his initiation he sang the opening credits of 'Olive et Tom' *(3)*, the Japanese animation where the hero is a young footballer. He was so at ease that he began things standing up before running around the tables.

Singing well is one thing, but playing well is even better. It's not a common thing for newbies, but I am picked from the start to play against Holland on March 5th, 2014, Erika's birthday. It shows the coach has confidence in me. 'La Marseillaise' made my heart vibrate. I was almost in tears when it began. In fact, when it was time for the anthems I looked up in order to banish any emotion and to avoid crying. There is no way I was going to look at my parents whom I'd spotted in the stands of the packed Stade de France during my warm-up.

I went into this game without any particular stress. I tried to do my best. Les Bleus went in 2-0 up at half-time, thanks to Karim Benzema and Blaise Matuidi. I had one chance to score but I failed to control the ball when I could have been straight through on Jasper Cillessen's goal. I was replaced by Loïc Rémy in the 68th minute. I only played six minutes with Franck Ribéry, who had just come on for Mathieu Valbuena. My first appearance, 16 days before my 23rd birthday, and on the date of Erika's: one hell of a day. I was happy with how I had played, considering the expectations. I wasn't very wasteful and I gave everything. *L'Équipe* gave me five out of ten with the following commentary: 'Can do better.' I never read the marks in the papers. I know very well when I have played well or put in an average performance.

I was hoping to make my mark because it was the last game before Deschamps was to announce his squad for Brazil. He had said to us before the match: "The door isn't closed, but the people who are here for this game have a good chance of being included." He had also told me that I should firstly try to enjoy the experience, to play as I do for my club and nothing else. After a few minutes had passed I had actually begun to feel better and better. I couldn't wait to have another taste of *Les Bleus*.

I wasn't playing my best football at Real Sociedad. The fans were beginning to have a go at me, implying that I was holding myself back for the national team. I didn't want my performances to drop. I don't work that way. But I wasn't the same player. I was different. I had put a lot of pressure on myself to make it when perhaps, even though I was feeling good physically, I wasn't quite as strong mentally. I was so hoping to figure among those 23! I had gone through a little bad patch, but I always gave everything for the club.

Éric Olhats thought I had done enough to be chosen. "In normal circumstances you'd be included," he told me, encouraging me to keep on working. I knew Deschamps would initially name a large squad but I wanted to be in that 23 and not on standby. I got my wish.

The coach announced his selection. I was at home in front of the TV and my heartbeat increased. When I saw my name and my photo on the screen as one of the six strikers I was jubilant again. I was both proud and relieved.

Thirty names had been put forward, the last seven of which were on standby and would accompany us to Brazil for our World Cup preparations. That was it: I was going to see Brazil, where I had never been before. I couldn't wait to prove the coach right.

(1) Nickname of the Germany national side, meaning 'The Team'.

(2) On January 18th, 2017, after almost three years of battling problems on his right ankle, he ended his career at only 25-years-old. Lyon, who signed him after the Under-20s World Cup, offered him a role at the club. After announcing his retirement because of "lacking the fitness to play football," Antoine Griezmann tweeted: "Thinking of my Bluets captain Gueïda Fofana. Wishing you all the best for the future."
(3) From the TV programme 'Captain Tsubasa'.

13

LESSONS FROM BRAZIL

We had three friendlies lined up before we left for South America so we could iron a few things out: against Norway at the Stade de France on May 27, 2014, against Paraguay on June 1st in Nice, and against Jamaica in Lille on June 8th. I was again a starter for the first game, giving way to Loïc Rémy in the 64th minute, who went on to score the third of our four goals. Five days later we were at the Allianz Riviera in front of the new stadium's record crowd of 35,200. On this occasion I started on the bench with my number 11. I came on in the 64th minute for Loïc Rémy, obviously.

Eighteen minutes later, I scored my first goal as a *Bleu.* It all started from a corner on the right which Olivier Giroud headed downwards from around the penalty spot. Laurent Koscielny threw himself to pull the ball back for me and from the left angle of the box I controlled it with my right – my bad foot – and curled in a shot. It sailed over the Paraguayan defence and into the corner of the net. As I got into position, my standing foot went back so much that I used less force than usual in my shot. It didn't matter because it ended up in the goal. The joy was huge. I slid on my knees to make the most of the moment and be as one with the fans, letting out cries of "Vamos! Vamos!" ("Come on! Come on!"). Victor Caceres' equalising header right at the end of the match didn't lessen my joy.

In the dressing room, all I wanted was to get back on the field. I didn't have to wait long because Jamaica were coming to the Pierre Mauroy Stadium in Villeneuve d'Ascq *(1)*. It was a real attacking fest, to which I contributed. We were already 6-0 up when I came on for Olivier Giroud in the 71st minute. I rounded off the exhibition with two more goals: the first from a pass by Karim Benzema and the second with a Madjer-style *(2)* back heel from Moussa Sissoko's cross.

It took us a 15 hour flight and one stop to reach Ribeirão Preto. It was in this town of 600,000 people, lying 300 kilometres north east of São Paulo, that the France team made its base camp. The Hotel JP – the Brazilians pronounced it 'Jotapé' – was completely at our disposal. It was decorated in blue, white and red colours and turned out to be comfortable and pleasant.

The staff waited on us hand and foot. They gave us a guard of honour and clapped us each time we came back in. The days were played out in good humour with training generally taking place in the afternoons, around 4pm. We spent a lot of time in the physio room, with the masseurs. It was an opportunity to chat, to laugh and also to watch the games. To pass the time I had brought my Xbox console and some TV series to slip into my DVD player. As the start of the competition approached, we also organised a big tournament of the FIFA video game on two televisions and with two groups. We each had a team. There was lots of shouting, often late at night, so much so that one day the coach asked us to stop because it was getting a bit out of hand and it could drain some of our energy. I have to say there was a lot of yelling.

We were in our bubble, relaxed and ambitious. On the night before our first game, Didier Deschamps informed me that I would be starting against Honduras. I was nervous. Usually I fall asleep easily, but on this occasion I went to ask the doctor for a tablet to help me drop off. I had a great sleep. I was so excited when I woke up the next day.

So I am picked to play behind Karim Benzema in Porto Alegre's Beira-Rio Stadium on June 15th, 2014. But our match begins with a hiccup: they didn't play our Marseillaise. We all looked at each other, speechless. The sound system had jammed at the time of the national anthems. A power failure! It may seem only a small matter but it was weird and, in truth, it ruined the enjoyment a little. Fortunately the 'Allons, enfants de la patrie' *(3)* could be heard from the stands, started by our supporters. So I got my Marseillaise! I had my first touch of the ball, then my second, then my third. I was feeling confident and in the rhythm. I think I started my World Cup well. I played the whole game, which we won 3-0 thanks to a Benzema double and an own goal.

Five days later, in Salvador, we were up against Switzerland, who were level with us at the top of Group E. France were leading 5-0 before the Swiss pulled a goal back in the 81st minute. I came on for Mathieu Valbuena a minute later. With six points from two games we were already through to the round of 16. I still chalked up 79 minutes against Ecuador in Rio's Maracana in a match which ended goalless. I did have the chance to open the scoring with a shot with the outside of my left foot but the keeper pushed it onto the post.

My parents were in Brazil, taking in every game *Les Bleus* played and making the most of the trip to do the tourist things. They returned to France as planned after the last group match. I managed to catch a glimpse of them just before the game against the South Americans. Didier Deschamps didn't really like us to be with our families in mid-competition. 'We're downstairs, if you've got the time to say hello,' is what they had sent me by text before we got on the bus in our suits to the stadium. The reunion lasted only a handful of seconds, just enough time for a look, but it was good to see them, right in the middle of the Tricolor fans.

So then it was Nigeria. If we lost we were out and going back home. The match took place in Brasília in a 70,000 capacity ultra-modern stadium, built for the World Cup. When we were nearing the arena it surged almost out of nowhere, on a huge axis off a motorway service area. The nearer we got to the stadium the more imposing it seemed. Its architecture was beautiful, and it was closed, which made it even more impressive. It was a 6pm kick-off and it was very hot, with the air particularly humid.

Karim Benzema came to talk to a few players during the warm-up. His encouraging words were hammered home with passion: "If we want to win, we're going to have to give everything." Karim is reserved and rather quiet. He can give the impression of being cold, as if he's not interested in other people, but that's not how it is. Even though he doesn't say much in front of the whole group, he does so with his team-mates when he feels the need. Karim is a cool guy, who enjoys a laugh and listening to music. He is also a monster when it comes to working, be it in training or in the gym. He constantly works on his finishing. He is an example, a really great striker, from whom I've got as many tips as possible, even though just watching him in training is instructive. Karim is the one I looked at with admiration when I used to go to Gerland, and I was often with him both on the field and in my time off it. I like to mix with him. It makes things easier.

I can't do this from the start in our round of 16 game because I'm on the bench. The match is tense, and so am I. I'm talking about it with two players who have the same attitude as me: Mickaël Landreau and Morgan Schneiderlin, who are sitting by my side. I'm right into this game, standing up when something dangerous happens. There are still no goals and the coach, through his assistant, Guy Stephan, asks me to warm up. The atmosphere is electric and the Brazilian public is clearly behind Nigeria.

I continue my sprints along the touchline, raising my head towards the bench to see if Didier Deschamps needs me. Not yet, so I carry on. Then I notice Guy Stephan waving me over: my time has come. My heart rate accelerates. I quickly remove my T-shirt and replace Olivier Giroud in the 62nd minute.

I hit a good shot with one of my first touches which Vincent Enyeama pushes away perfectly for a corner. It's game on! In the 79th minute we finally make the breakthrough when Paul Pogba heads into an empty net after a Mathieu Valbuena corner had been badly cleared. Five minutes later, I create a good chance behind the Nigerian defence but the keeper pushes out my left foot shot with his right hand. However, he is powerless when we move into stoppage time. Valbuena and

Benzema play a quick short corner, with the former sending over a low cross to the near post. I want to intercept the centre but the Nigeria defender, Joseph Yobo, whom I've got the better of, gets the final touch of the ball and puts it past his own team-mate. We are in the quarter-finals, which had been the objective set by the president of the Federation. We went over to thank our fans. The dream was still alive. Next opponents: Germany. Our nemesis. Among the squad, we were convinced that if we managed to beat them we would go all the way.

When we were approaching the Maracana in the bus, I was able to see in the distance the big statue of Christ the Redeemer, high on Corcovado mountain. That's all the tourist stuff! The Maracana may be a beautiful place to end your days but we had no intention of doing so.

We are confident about our game. I'm preferred to Oliver Giroud in attack. At 0-0 I'm given a good ball, but instead of shooting I try to find Karim Benzema. Today, with my experience, when I'm in this type of situation I don't mess about: I shoot. Deschamps had reminded us the day before the game to pay attention to set pieces, insisting that the Germans were very effective in that area. We knew that, but it didn't stop Toni Kroos from delivering a free-kick wide from the left in the 13th minute for Mats Hummels to beat Raphaël Varane to the ball and head past Hugo Lloris.

We knew straight away that getting back on terms would be difficult. We give everything we have, creating a few chances. The German defence holds out and their goalkeeper, Manuel Neuer, as he had done since the start of the World Cup, is colossal. He stops everything. We have the impression that the match could go on for hours and we still wouldn't be able to score. I keep calling for the ball to be played forwards and I make diagonal runs. But nothing seems to work. In stoppage time Benzema must only be on the edge of the six yard box and from a tight angle Neuer blocks his powerful shot with his wrist without seeming to move, leaving us stunned. Totally sickening. We had deserved to equalise, but there you go, the Germans will go to the semis.

I can't hold back my tears. Sobs of release. I didn't score during this World Cup, playing on the left side as for my club, but too far from the goal. But I got incredible enjoyment in doing what I'm good at, knowing how to play one-twos or working between the lines, always moving, rather than taking people on and crossing.

Leaving my friends was going to be tricky. We had spent some marvellous times together, honestly. The atmosphere was idyllic. I can't count the number of times where we put the world to rights after dinner. I can't remember one blow up. The only friction came from the people who had lost mini-games in training. Everyone pulled their weight. We listened to the leaders, Lloris and Evra. Hugo, the captain, can seem mild but you shouldn't go by appearances. He rarely speaks, but when he does everyone listens. As for Patrice, he's more of the winding-up kind. He keeps the squad together. He's always talking, and he goads us a bit during the warm-ups.

Pat is 10 years older than me, having started with *Les Bleus* in 2004. I had a few concerns when I turned up for the first time. As many people do, I had an image of someone who took himself very seriously and who can unsettle a group. It's a label borne out of his captaincy in the previous World Cup in South Africa. The Patrice Evra I mixed with was nothing of the sort. He was constantly bantering in the dressing room, instilling a good mood. I was next to him in Clairefontaine and was often the butt of his jokes. But he became serious on the field and he was the first one to give me advice on my positioning. A really good surprise. And what a career! His humour is deadly, and he gave nicknames to us all. It's he who first called me 'Grizou', and it's stayed with me.

When it came to my generation, I was also often with Paul Pogba and Raphaël Varane. Raph is younger than me but he is very mature and calm. When I took my first steps with *Les Bleus* he was protective towards me and was reassuring. We spoke often and when it came to working in twos in training we were regularly together. Paul is like me. He likes to laugh and mess around, but also to sing and dance; there, however, I'm not quite as at ease. I'm more PlayStation, him not so much.

Over time, Paul became a true friend. I've told him that if he had a day or two free in Manchester he could come and visit me in Madrid and get to know Erika and the little one, about whom I speak to him a lot. He is part of the family. In Brazil, the defeat by Germany got to him, too. We didn't want to head back home, but we had to. In the first few days I would go over the game time and time again, especially as people were only talking about *Les Bleus* on the television.

In Mâcon I watched our tormentors beat Argentina in the final, then I went on holiday with my relatives to Turkey. I tried to disconnect, but it wasn't easy especially as my transfer to Atlético Madrid was being negotiated. In short, these were not totally relaxing holidays. There were a lot of questions going through my mind.

Even though many observers considered me to be the French revelation of this World Cup because of the freshness

I brought, I didn't feel that way. I still didn't feel an important part of this team. I would often play for an hour and frequently be the first one to come off. I took everything the coach gave me and I tried to show what I could do in training. I was losing my way because, in my first games for Atlético I had to settle for playing bits of matches. I wanted to raise the level of my game because I still wasn't at my best. I was neither invaluable to my club nor my national team.

On September 4th, 2014, ten days after making the assist for Mario Mandzukic to score the Spanish Supercup winner against Real Madrid, I made my 10th appearance for France against Spain, whom we hadn't beaten for ten years. The Stade de France was full to bursting. It was our first appearance since the World Cup quarter-final.

I began the match but I stayed on the pitch for less than an hour. Loïc Rémy came on for me and scored the only goal. Playing against Spain, which had adopted me from my 14th year and who had been World Champions four years earlier, should have motivated me. But I wasn't at it. Against *La Roja (4)* who fielded Sergio Ramos, Sergio Busquets and Cesc Fabregas, I hardly got a kick. I was out of it, although four days later we had to play another friendly in Belgrade. We had planned to go to Serbia the day after our win against Spain, following a final training session at the Stade de France.

After it was over, Didier Deschamps asked me to come and see him in the dressing room. He wanted to have a little chat. Right from the start, he said: "So what's up? Don't you want to play? Don't you want to be in the French team?"

Then he added: "Tell me if you have a problem with the squad or with me because, I'm telling you straight, you were useless yesterday!"

I took it in and I replied: "Coach, I don't need reminding. I know I was useless. That wasn't me out on the field! I didn't touch the ball, I didn't attack and I didn't defend."

It was a frank conversation. The coach continued and warned me: "Antoine, if it carries on like this you're not going to play much." I reassured him, stating that it wouldn't happen again and that I would do my best to live up to his expectations and also my own. Deschamps was right to clear the air and to play the truth card, even if it wasn't pleasant to hear. He was doing his job. Anyway, I was aware I wasn't in the groove.

I appreciated our talk. I'd rather that than him benching me without any explanation. To be sure that the message had got through, the match in Partizan Belgrade's stadium was my second wake-up call. I was a substitute and the coach changed two thirds of his team.

I began to warm up on the hour. Karim Benzema had just come on for Loïc Rémy. I wasn't among the first three people to warm up so in my mind I wasn't going to play. But I carried on with my exercises.

Rémy Cabella came off for Alexandre Lacazette and then Blaise Matuidi for Paul Pogba. There were only two of us left warming up. In the 82nd minute Mathieu Valbuena replaced Moussa Sissoko, two minutes after the Manchester City defender, Aleksandar Kolarov, had equalised with a free-kick. I sat back down again. I equated this to a merciless punishment. But I understand what he did. I wasn't going through my best period and there is no doubt I wasn't focused enough on *Les Bleus*.

Deschamps' attitude and words made me think. And they got me back on the right track. They had to: the Euros at home were in our sights.

(1) Part of the European Metropolis of Lille.
(2) The French often refer to such a goal as a 'Madjer', in tribute to former Algeria striker Rabah Madjer, who scored an equaliser with a memorable back heel for FC Porto in their 1987 European Cup final victory over Bayern Munich.
(3) "Let's go, children of the Fatherland." The first line of 'La Marseillaise'.
(4) Nickname of the Spanish national team.

14

A PLAYER'S WORST ENEMY

I am resistant to pressure. In fact, I thrive on it so it doesn't get to me. I don't pay attention to everything about my sport. The only pressure I've known was at the birth of my Mia. Since Erika was having a caesarean I was afraid for her and for the baby. I didn't know what to do. I was helpless. That's not the case on the field! I've known football since I was very small and there's nothing it can teach me and there's nothing about it which can surprise me. Football is still a game. A game I strive to enjoy.

After a striker has missed a chance who among us, in a stadium or in front of their TV, hasn't come out with: "Why didn't he put it away? Why didn't he side-foot it? Why didn't he pass it to him instead of shooting?" And I'm being polite there!

I know every one of these sentences which are hurled spontaneously because I myself, in front of my telly, am a fan of the beautiful game and of goals. I'm the first to say what would have been the best thing to do.

What is not known, however, is how a striker has been able to miss 'a sitter'. I went through this kind of rough patch at the end of 2016. Here's the proof: I hadn't scored in La Liga for 843 minutes! It was long, far too long. Goalless in the league for nine consecutive games since the start of October, I found the net again on January 7th away to Eibar. I had also scored four days earlier, but it was in the King's Cup (Copa del Rey), against Las Palmas.

The mind is a footballer's worst enemy. I'm speaking from experience. At the start of December when we came up against Bayern Munich in the Champions League, I was right in the middle of an insecure period, where things weren't happening for me in front of goal.

We had beaten Bayern 1-0 in our Group D match at the end of September, Yannick Ferreira Carrasco scoring the winner from one of my passes, while a bit later on I fired a penalty against the bar. There was nothing at stake in the game in Bavaria on December 6th, we were guaranteed to finish first in the group and Bayern were assured of second place. When we were in our hotel in Munich the day before, I didn't know if I was going to be playing considering the fixture wouldn't change anything, even though there would be some pride in winning at Bayern and ending our group matches unbeaten.

A meeting is planned that evening at 10.30pm, after the meal. I'm guessing it will just be between the players, because we weren't in the best position in the league. I get to the room at 10.29pm, already feeling a little stressed. I'm thinking: 'Shit, I'm going to be the last one and they're going to be waiting for me.' It wasn't my fault, it was Football Manager's! I see when

I go in that we are not alone. The coaching staff are also there: the coach himself, Diego Simeone, whom we all call 'El Cholo' *(1)*, his assistant German Burgos, as well as Pablo Vercellone the goalkeeping coach, the fitness coach Oscar Ortega, while not forgetting Simeone's other assistant, Juan Vizcaíno, a former Atlético Madrid player. I look to see where 'my' South Americans are. I find them and I take my place next to Angel Correa and Miguel Moyà. The meeting begins.

The coach speaks first. Then it's the turn of Diego Godín. Fernando Torres, Koke and Nico Gaitán follow him. I'm wondering when Diego Simeone is going to pitch in.

"And you, Antoine, how are you feeling?" My time comes after a few minutes' wait. I haven't scored for six games in La Liga, I'm aware that I'm not helping my team win. I begin with: "I'm going to speak personally of how I'm feeling." I'm off. "I'm not happy on the field, I'm not enjoying it."

What I've just said is strong. Cholo stops me on this and asks: "But do you know why?" He answers for me. "You are putting too many things in your head." To which I reply: "I think I'm playing or thinking in a selfish way, and I hate it. I get pissed off when you tell me to play on the right. I get pissed off when you tell me to play near the box."

I use the following example: "The other day, I came back to get a touch of the ball and Gabi said to me: 'No, don't come so deep, stay higher up'. I told him to sod off, saying that he should leave me free to do what I wanted. I do what you ask, I move forward and I go near to goal. But, from time to time, I need to come back again. I think it's just a mental thing for me, that's all. I am going to carry on working and giving everything, as always."

I got it all off my chest. Everyone said their piece, about how they all viewed the situation. It was important to talk, to know everybody's opinion and not be overwhelmed by things which are unsaid.

I'm mentioning this incident because it makes people realise that a striker who isn't fully confident can't necessarily score. When he is crippled with doubt he will hit the post despite being completely unmarked and the keeper is already on the ground, and he's pleading: "Please score!"

I enjoyed that meeting, where everybody spoke frankly. Of course, the next day we lost 1-0 to Bayern. But I was pleased to have put my troubles into words, to have got across what I was feeling, to have gone over my short period of ineffectiveness.

Three days before Munich we had produced a 0-0 home draw against Espanyol in the league. Ahead of the meeting, our Uruguayan fitness coach, Oscar Ortega, whom we called 'El Profe' *(2)*, had put on a short training session especially for the strikers. The exercise was thus: eight shots at the middle of the goal, four from a tight angle on the left and four from a tight angle on the right. My result: a nice seven out of eight in the middle, one out of two on the left side and one out of four on the right. Basically, I was on fire! I even took the liberty of mocking our goalkeeper, the Slovenian Jan Oblak, who was very touchy. Kevin Gameiro and I gave him some gentle ribbing.

That was fine except that, against Espanyol, I was given three clear chances and I didn't make an impression in front of goal. But that certainly made an impression on me!

I could and should have helped my team win. Why didn't the ball want to go in? Players are the only ones who can understand. I wasn't in the game mentally. I didn't find myself concentrating one hundred per cent. In reality I was pissed off because the coach had put me on the right. I was pissed off because Gabi had asked me not to drop back. I realised that I wasn't enjoying it and I was sulking. It's a little of what I spoke about at the meeting in Munich.

Against Espanyol, when I get the ball from Gaitán and I find myself alone in front of goal, I'm not in the best frame of mind to score. I'm just ready to shoot and wait to see what happens. That's not my game. No, I'm not ready to shoot and 'kill' the keeper as I should be. As it happens I shoot with the inside of my foot. It's a soft shot which Diego López saves without exerting himself.

Generally, if you give me the same chance when I'm enjoying myself on the field, I'm already doing my 'Hotline Bling' to celebrate the goal!

Football is certainly played with your legs, but mainly it's played with your head…

(1) Loosely translates as 'half-breed'.

(2) The Teacher.

15

TRAGEDY IN PARIS

It took me a while to establish my place in the France team. While the World Cup in Brazil was rewarding, it didn't mean I was an automatic choice. In the aftermath, following my average performance against Spain and my remaining on the bench in Serbia, I was given a starting role against Portugal at the Stade de France in October 2014. Morgan Schneiderlin came on for me six minutes from time in a 2-1 win. In another friendly against Armenia in Yerevan three days later, *Les Bleus* won 3-0. This would be the case right up to the Euros for which, as the host country, France had automatically qualified.

I got onto the field in Armenia in the second half. Controlling a forward pass down the middle from André-Pierre Gignac in the 84th minute, I beat the keeper with two touches before scoring in the empty net. That's enough to get your confidence back. But we didn't have the chance to catch our breath because in mid-November Albania came to play us in Rennes. They were tough opponents and they were ahead at half-time. Didier Deschamps sent me on for Yohan Cabaye just before the hour. In the 73rd minute, released by Christophe Jallet down the right, I broke through the defence and let fly with a powerful low left foot shot which the keeper couldn't stop.

The year ended at Marseille's Stade Vélodrome with a narrow victory over Sweden, who were without the injured Zlatan Ibrahimović. The winning goal in Marseille came from Raphaël Varane who, as captain for the night, headed in my left wing corner. I played the whole of the game. That took my total to 14 appearances in nine months, with five goals. It was a more than respectable ratio – I was, for example, ahead of Thierry Henry and David Trezeguet over the same period – especially as I was mainly playing out wide.

What was interesting was the fact that my five goals had all been scored after I had come on. I was able to benefit from the opponents' tiredness, even if I was obviously off the pace of the game, by bringing my liveliness. That's how you get perceived as a super-sub. It's simple: Over the nine matches I'd started so far I hadn't scored a goal in 698 minutes, while when coming off the bench I'd hit five in 142 minutes!

The risk of being reduced to the role of a luxury substitute was there, someone who could be pulled out of the hat when the situation called for it. That's not what I was looking for. Winding me up, the coach had a pop along the lines of: "If you carry on like that you won't be starting another game but you'll always be our substitute." It was said with a smile because I showed I could be effective when called upon, but that's not what I wanted. My ambition was to cement my place in the starting eleven, to become one of the big players in the squad.

I had my heart set on showing that I wasn't just a replacement. I'm someone who loves getting involved and who likes the freedom of the field. But I was trying to find myself, especially as Karim Benzema was the man down the middle for *Les Bleus*, while Diego Simeone asked me to play there at Atlético Madrid. I gave everything for the national team, I did my best. But I still hadn't produced my benchmark game.

The start of the 2015 internationals didn't, from that point of view, move things forward. In March, *Les Bleus* went down 3-1 to Neymar and Thiago Silva's Brazil in the Stade de France. Didier Deschamps may have picked me from the start in that match, but he took me off a quarter of an hour from the end. My performance wasn't mind-blowing and it was all the more unfortunate that I had already scored 14 goals in La Liga for Atlético. Three days later, on March 29th in Saint-Étienne, I played the first hour down the left side against Denmark. Before the summer arrived I had come off at half-time in the Stade de France against Belgium, who put four past us (4-3). Then, a week after that, I stayed on for an hour in Tirana against Albania. Despite these two defeats the atmosphere remained upbeat.

From the beginning, I had got on particularly well with Paul Pogba. We were always together when we were with the national team. We speak a lot during the season, we send each other photos via Snapchat. He, too, is very family orientated, with a ubiquitous mother and two brothers who are also footballers. He, too, likes to laugh and to set the mood. He, too, left home very young: a native of Seine-en-Marne, he joined Le Havre when he was 14, then Manchester United two years later.

Paul is a great guy. Because of his over-exposure in the media, his transfer fee and his spectacular style of play, everything he does is scrutinised. All the lights are trained on him. The press is very demanding with him, sometimes too harsh in my opinion. You can get the feeling that everything just slides off him, but it's not the case. I suggested that he shouldn't pay too much attention to what's said about him and that he should just get his head down. He is such a hard worker, a remarkable player. And he's someone who needs to feel loved. The media, even though they are doing their job, should encourage this more. People shouldn't forget that he's only young. He doesn't get the recognition he deserves. Paul has the potential to win the Ballon d'Or one day.

I began France's game against Portugal on the bench at Lisbon's José Alvalade Stadium on September 4th, 2015. But I came on earlier than had been planned: Nabil Fekir damaged his cruciate knee ligaments in the 14th minute. He collapsed after injuring himself and would subsequently be out for many months. I leapt off the bench to replace him and be part of what was an encouraging win. I was sad for Nabil, whom I like. In fact, when he would make his return with *Les Bleus* in October 2016, I would pose next to him for a photo in the dressing room wearing his number 12 shirt.

Three days after Lisbon, we welcomed Serbia to Bordeaux. Blaise Matuidi scored our two goals and I played the entire match, or virtually: the coach took me off in the 90th minute. Our journey towards the Euros gathered pace against Armenia in Nice on October 8th. I had already scored there against Paraguay, and I did so again at the Allianz Riviera. Following a one-two with Karim Benzema in the 35th minute, I let fly with a strong right foot shot from inside the area, and the ball went through the keeper's legs.

It was my first goal for *Les Bleus* for a year, and my first one in a game which I had started. After 21 appearances it was about time! Three days later, through a brace from Olivier Giroud, we beat Denmark 2-1 in Copenhagen. Mathieu Valbuena replaced me 12 minutes from time. We had two prestige fixtures coming up in the next month: the visit of the German World Champions and a trip to Wembley against England.

The Stade de France provided a nice setting for the reception of Germany, on that November 13th, 2015. My parents were in the stands. I was chosen to start – it was becoming a habit – alongside Olivier Giroud and Anthony Martial. The pitch wasn't in a very good condition. So, of course, *Les Bleus* chalk up a fifth consecutive victory and I play for 90 minutes until Hatem Ben Arfa comes on for me.

But what significance does this match have in the light of the terrible drama which was happening at the same time around the stadium and at the Bataclan Theatre? None, of course…

From the pictures, shortly after the first quarter of the game, we could see Patrice Evra's eyes open wide when he made a back pass, as if he was wondering what was going on. He was positioned near the East Stand and he heard some sort of an explosion. But, as we all did, he thought it was a flare or large firecrackers. There were smoke bombs and the atmosphere was friendly. We didn't hear the commotion which was around or the police sirens.

We returned to the dressing room at half-time, just as we normally did. Everything was unclear. The instructions were that we were not to be told. For example, we didn't know that the President of the Republic, who was made aware that there had been multiple shootings in the heart of Paris, had been led away from the Stade de France. Just as I didn't pay attention to the helicopter which was flying over the arena.

At the end of the game, the match announcer spoke of an 'incident' outside. When we were in the tunnel we saw pictures on the screen about there being a hostage situation.

We became aware of what was happening, even though we still didn't realise the full significance. But, very quickly, the fear increased as we watched the news channels live, when we were able to pick up snippets. Naturally, the press conferences and the walk through the mixed zone were cancelled. We were not allowed to leave.

I knew that Maud, who is a music buff, was attending a concert in Paris. I called my mum, who was in the stands with my dad.

"Where's Maud?" I asked.

"At a concert of I don't know who, but it's not at the Bataclan," she replied assuredly.

I insisted, as if I'd had a premonition: "Give me the name of the band…"

"It's a rock group," my mum answers.

I replied sharply: "I know it: I know it's the group which is playing at the Bataclan," as it happens Eagles of Death Metal.

I tried to reach Maud. She didn't answer. I left messages. I went to get a shower. The telly was off in the dressing room. I quickly joined my parents in the players' lounge.

They confirmed that my sister was at the Bataclan with a friend. We were very, very scared. We were filled with anxiety. It was impossible to know if she was okay.

Eventually she picked up.

Maud spoke in a low voice and then the conversation was cut off. Once again there was no reply from her phone. She managed to call her mum very late into the night to explain that she had got out after the security forces intervened. She had taken refuge in a restaurant with other survivors while the police were carrying out their operations inside. The relief was extreme. I thank the man upstairs.

The evening was tough, endless. Maud was safe and sound, and so were all the Griezmanns. She ran as fast as she could when she was able to leave the Bataclan, taking off her shoes so she could go even quicker. It was almost two o'clock in the morning. She wanted to get a taxi but they didn't stop. They refused to take her because she was covered in blood, that of the injured and of the dead bodies, and they didn't want their seats to get stained. She finally managed to hail one in the Place de la République. Once at home she took a long shower.

We players had been discharged to Clairefontaine at nearly 3am. There, with Hugo Lloris, Dimitri Payet and the others, we rushed to the TVs. That's when we became fully aware of the battle scenes which had marked Paris. Still in a state of shock, the Germans chose to spend the night in the dressing room and then head directly to the airport.

I'm a bit reticent and so I haven't really spoken much to Maud about the tragic evening of November 13th. She, too, has kept a low profile *(1)*, which I completely understand.

We always think this sort of thing will only ever happen to others. That is not the case. She could have been killed. We had to get ourselves back together. Maud spent a few days at my home in Madrid, as did my parents. I didn't expand much on the subject. I did, however, tweet, to reassure everyone: 'Thanks to God my sister got out of the Bataclan. All my prayers go to the victims and their families.'

These attacks, which were claimed by Daesh *(2)*, were the

bloodiest in France's history, with 130 dead and hundreds more wounded.

Among the victims was Asta Diakité, while she was in her car. She was the cousin of Lassana Diarra who, at that moment, had been on the pitch against Germany at the Stade de France. He shared his sadness on social media and wanted to pay tribute to her. In a moving and pertinent message, Lass wrote:

> *Following yesterday's dramatic events in Paris and Saint Denis, I am speaking today with a heavy heart. As you may have read, I have been personally affected by these attacks. My cousin, Asta Diakité, was among the victims of one of the shootings which took place yesterday, as were hundreds of other innocent French people. She was someone I looked up to, a support, a big sister. In this climate of terror it is important for all of us, who are representatives of our country and its diversity, to speak up and stand united in the face of a horror which has no colour or religion. Together let us defend love, respect and peace. Thank you to all of you for your tributes and your messages. Take care of yourselves and your own, and may our victims rest in peace.*

It goes without saying that four days after such a shockwave, we had no desire to go to Wembley. "Why play football at this time? It's pointless…" Such was the state of my thoughts. I'd have preferred to be with my sister than with *Les Bleus*. But the Federation decided that the game should go ahead.

To mark the occasion, if that's the right expression, the anthem 'God Save The Queen' echoed out before ours. 'La

Marseillaise' which followed was particularly moving, sung together by the French and English fans. Then the 90,000 spectators respected wonderfully the minute of silence which preceded the kick-off. I thought about Maud and all of the victims again. This November 17th was not a day for football…

For the record, France lost in London and I came on in the 67th minute. Lassana Diarra got on ten minutes earlier. He was dignified. He was angry during the get-together, but he always kept his calm. He never lost it in front of us.

Life began to run its course again, as well as it could. On a much more selfish level, I had nothing to complain about. I was brimming with confidence ahead of France's next game in Amsterdam on March 25th, 2016. I was flying with Atlético Madrid, especially in the Champions League, and Erika was pregnant. For me, who needs to be happy in my daily life in order to perform well on the field, it was perfect. Because I had been used a lot by my club, I only played the first half. But it was enough for me to register my eighth goal in Blue, in the sixth minute, from a free-kick which I had won. I was a little over 20 metres from goal, to the right of the area, and my left foot shot ended up high in the net on the opposite side.

I opted for a different celebration, inspired by the one of my Madrid team-mate Fernando Torres. My goal chilled the atmosphere of an Ajax Arena which was full of emotion following the passing of the Dutch football idol, Johan Cruyff, the previous day.

Four days afterwards Russia came to the Stade de France, where we hadn't played since the November attacks. It was our final game before the squad for the Euros was announced. I played a good hour, enough time to make an assist for

N'Golo Kanté and another for André-Pierre Gignac. The 4-2 win proved the extent, if proof was needed, of our attacking potential.

My life became complete in April with the birth of my daughter Mia. In that same month Karim Benzema won't be so lucky. He announced in a tweet on the 13th: 'Unfortunately for me and for all those who have backed and supported me, I won't be chosen for our Euros in France.'

The French Federation would confirm it in a press release *(3)*. I was disappointed for Karim. The legal soap opera, which the political world helped increase its exposure, was commented on a lot. Too much. But this unrest didn't disturb *Les Bleus*. Of course the fact that two team-mates were involved didn't make it easy to bear. I would have been thrilled for Karim and Mathieu (Valbuena) to take part in the tournament but, as is only to be expected, the players were not consulted. To be honest, I was mostly thinking about myself, how I could be in top form for the Euros and, in the meantime, continue to advance in the Champions League. I was completely focused on my game and nothing else.

Considering Karim's media attention and status, I knew that his absence would put greater pressure on the shoulders of Paul Pogba and me. Didier Deschamps announced his squad for the Euros the following month. Gone was the suspense I had had before the 2014 World Cup. This time I knew I'd be in.

Dimitri Payet, Anthony Martial, Kingsley Coman, Olivier Giroud and André-Pierre Gignac made up the other strikers. To those 23, the coach added eight players on stand-by: Alphonse Areola, Haten Ben Arfa, Kevin Gameiro, Alexandre Lacazette, Adrien Rabiot, Morgan Schneiderlin, Djibril

Sidibé and Samuel Umtiti. Because of the Champions League final, I met up with the squad immediately afterwards for their get-together in Austria, just ten days before the opening game. I played a half against Scotland in Metz on June 4th, and joined my team-mates again, who defeated Cameroon without me in Nantes. It was a good warm-up period.

In the run-up to the Euros, there were a lot of questions about my fitness when I joined up with *Les Bleus*. I had indeed played an extended season, taking part in 54 games with my club, making 63 in total. I understand that such a figure can make an impression. Some people even had fun calculating the number of kilometres I ran in the Champions League: more than 142 in 13 games, the second highest in the competition behind my Atlético captain, Gabi. I didn't feel especially exhausted and I managed my recovery so I could start each game in the best possible state. I couldn't wait for it to begin.

We didn't spend the night before the opening match at Clairefontaine, our base camp, but in a hotel in Bercy, UEFA's rules stipulating that we were not allowed to be more than 60 kilometres from the stadium before this kind of fixture. A big show was broadcast on TV at the foot of the Eiffel Tower. We all watched it and we loved it. I tweeted: 'You can turn the music down, David Guetta. I can't sleep. #GreatShow.' I wanted to play and I kept smiling, even though, naturally, I hadn't come to terms with the loss of a Champions League final a few days earlier and hitting the crossbar with a penalty. While I had to look ahead to the game against Romania, I couldn't help dwelling on all that. I was seeing the ball rebound off the bar again, not cross the line and going out the other side. I was a hair's breadth away from getting my hands on the Cup ... I had to get out of the doldrums.

I began against Romania. The opening match in the Stade de France on June 10th wasn't scintillating. It went to the wire and Dimitri Payet snatched the victory. I watched his superb left foot strike from the bench. I was no longer on the pitch: I was the first *Bleu* to have been withdrawn by Didier Deschamps in the 66th minute. I'd had the chance to open the scoring after a quarter of an hour on a cross from Bacary Sagna, but my header, which was made after a rebound, ended up against the post.

That header from point-blank range showed that, mentally, I wasn't in top form. Normally that type of ball hits the back of the net ... I was happy for Dim, who couldn't hold back tears after his goal. We suffered, but the important thing was getting the win. There had been suspense and commitment; the ideal training scenario for everyone and for getting the public warmed up!

We were in a cocoon at Clairefontaine. Outside of training we would watch the other games on a big screen in the video room. I did some muscle building exercises on my legs. Some chose to stay quiet in their room, others played Perudo, a Chilean dice game. I don't eat breakfast, but on entering the room on June 13th I saw the papers as I did every day, spread under the mirror opposite.

There was a big headline on the front page: 'The Griezmann concern.' The photo showed me on my haunches with the France shirt on my back, staring into space. As a reference to the two inside pages which were devoted to this 'case file' it was written: *As the heralded leader of the France team, the Atlético Madrid striker was very quiet against Romania (2-1), on Friday. Should we be worried?*

As I've said before, I took that very badly. I thought: 'Ah, the bastards!' I didn't need this. Not right now, after Romania, after the defeat in the Champions League final and a season of over 60 games. I gave everything for my country and that's how I get treated in return? It's impossible to be bullet-proof when it comes to this sort of thing. My dad, who reads all the papers, was affected. And, in turn, so was I.

I knew very well that I hadn't performed in my first game of the Euros. I was looking ahead to our next opponent, Albania, at the Stade Vélodrome in Marseille on June 15th. I wanted to make amends.

The night before the game, or maybe even the morning of it, I can't really remember, the coach showed up in my room. He said that he had made a choice, explaining that I was going to start on the bench. He told me that it wasn't a punishment and that I was definitely going to come on. My first reaction was to go and find Paul Pogba and tell him about it, to which he replied: "It's the same for me!"

Deschamps' role is about determining things, finding the best formula in a 23-man squad. Of course people were going to be disappointed every time. He was doing his job. It was a disappointment knowing that Paul and I were not going to be playing from the start. I had the feeling somewhere that the journalists from *L'Équipe* hadn't as much helped us as crushed us. They were tough on us. It was hard to swallow, even though we believed that we were going to get on. I'm not saying that the coach bowed to media pressure, but let's just say that that front page didn't do us any favours, as the TV stations almost exclusively focused their attention on Paul and me.

The situation was a bit hard to take. But things worked out well for both of us. He was brought on at half-time and I replaced Kingsley Coman in the 68th minute when the score was 0-0. And it was me who rescued *Les Bleus* – and myself as well – in the 90th minute with a downward header across goal from Adil Rami's centre from the right. How sweet that was! My first goal in a European Championship. Me, who hadn't scored in the World Cup! I was ecstatic. Towards the end of stoppage time Dimitri Payet's curled shot made the victory, which had taken a long time to acquire, more emphatic. This second win in as many games took us into the round of 16.

In order to guarantee first place in the group, we needed to avoid defeat against Switzerland on June 19th at the Stade Pierre Mauroy in Villeneuve-d'Ascq. Paul and I were in the starting line-up again for this crazy match with loads of chances. He played all of it and hit the bar with a shot. As for me, I came off in the 77th minute, replaced by Blaise Matuidi. I could have opened the scoring but the goalkeeper made a good save from my right-foot shot, following a one-two with André-Pierre Gignac: I'd fired too near the middle of the goal. Both teams ended the game on good terms with a goalless draw. There were no injuries and we hadn't used up too much energy: a perfect result. I felt good, and I knew I was getting stronger.

We had to wait to find out who our next opponent was. We thought it was going to be Northern Ireland, but in the end it would be the Republic of Ireland who, by beating Italy, finished third in their group behind Germany and Poland. The clash was scheduled for Lyon in the new Parc OL. Needless to say we were favourites against a team whose players all played in England except for the veteran Robbie Keane, who was plying his trade in America. Naturally Olivier Giroud found himself leading the line again with me on the right flank and Dimitri Payet opposite.

Kick-off was set for 3pm on Sunday, June 26th, in bright sunshine. Except that very quickly the weather turned stormy. In the second minute Paul fouled the Southampton striker, Shane Long, in the box. When the referee pointed to the penalty spot I said to myself: "No, not now! If he scores it's going to be hard to come back."

Robbie Brady put it away. We had been caught cold and we were struggling to react. We couldn't create any danger. No clear-cut chance came our way, while the heat was increasing. I had no idea again that at half-time Didier Deschamps would take a radical step.

A step which would prove decisive for my Euro and my career in Blue, proving that I was able to become the player I wanted to be.

(1) Maud Griezmann made an exception for the New York Times and for L'Équipe, confiding to the latter: "In fact, November 13th is a day I want him to forget. Him and the other members of my family. Up till then nobody had been aware that he had a sister, which didn't bother him at all. On the contrary. I had my life and he his. (...) When Antoine saw me again for the first time, a little less than a week afterwards, he said to me: "I feel as if nothing has happened to you." In fact, I didn't want to show that I was affected. For me, I wasn't a victim because I was neither injured nor dead. So we had to move forward. (...) Even so, I was stuck inside for over an hour and a half. I know that my parents and my brothers were really worried at first. Later they realised that I was going through my own personal therapy by being an arsehole and by talking openly to my mates about it."

(2) So-called Islamic State.
(3) "The president and the coach would like to point out that sporting performance is an important but not an exclusive criterion regarding selection for the France team. The capacity of players to work towards unity, within and around the group, exemplary behaviour and the safeguarding of the squad are also taken into account by all the coaches of the Federation. As a result Noël Le Graët and Didier Deschamps have decided that Karim Benzema will not be able to participate in Euro 2016." Benzema had been charged in November 2015 for "aiding and abetting a blackmail attempt" and for "participation in a criminal association" relating to an alleged sex tape blackmail against Mathieu Valbuena, an allegation he denied.

16

EDGE OF GLORY

I pay attention to every move I make, never forgetting to smile at the fans. That's not the only reason why I'm popular with youngsters *(1)*. But it's part of the job. And above all, I like it. Occasionally, however, I give myself a break from this, especially when I'm on holiday.

So in the summer of 2014, after our elimination in the quarter-finals of the World Cup in Brazil, I went to Turkey with all my family, to Club Med. I was hoping to unwind, to rest and to enjoy the company of the people close to me. I was able to notice that I was really starting to be recognised outside of Spain. The requests, while always good natured, were endless. They became tiresome because I was there to get some rest and, mortified by our defeat by Germany (1-0), I just wanted to forget everything.

I knew that my future was in the process of being decided. I wanted to leave Real Sociedad. I reckoned I'd gone as far as I could. I felt the need to experience something else, to feel challenged, to fight every week for my place, to play the

Champions League and to be at the top of the table each season. When it came to the next destination it was up to Éric Olhats to take care of the sports side of things. He began to show urgency because two weeks later I was to begin training at Zubieta. Of course I could still leave even after pre-season had begun but I wanted the transfer to be sorted out beforehand. I couldn't imagine myself training with a team I wanted to leave.

I was still in Turkey when Éric called. Real Sociedad had set my release clause at 30 million euros. "Antoine, we've got Tottenham interested. They are ready to pay 20 million pounds, around 25 million euros. But I don't know if the Real president is going to accept that. They're discussing it together. And you, would you like to go there or do you prefer to hang on?" Tottenham Hotspur is one of the London clubs, now coached by the Argentinian Mauricio Pochettino. I didn't want to rush into anything or to get carried away. "Let's wait for them to agree first. Then we'll see," I replied.

A new club became interested with every passing day. But none of them put forward a good offer. Or, to be more precise, none made a concrete offer. I was carrying on sunning myself when the phone rang again. It was Éric.

"Hello, Antoine, how are you? I've had a call from Atlético Madrid. And this is very serious. They are very keen. What do you think?"

I was enthusiastic. But I had one concern: the coach, Diego Simeone. Not least his explosive nature. "That may work, but the coach is crazy, right?" I asked Éric. I was very tempted. I added: "I really like the team, they're in the Champions League and they're still going to be looking at the top places! We've got to go for it, and Atlético have got to make an offer to Real Sociedad. If the club accepts I will meet them."

I opened up to Erika about this. "I'll let you handle the football side, of course, and I trust you," she said. "As for the city, I think I'll like Madrid. It's the capital and I've got a girlfriend there, so don't worry about me." But something was bothering her. "On the other hand, I'm worried about the reaction of the Real fans." I shared her doubts. I have a lot of respect for them. They have always been behind me and never whistled. I was hoping they would understand my decision.

After my discussion with Erika, I made contact with my Real team-mate, the Uruguayan Gonzalo Castro Irizábal – or 'Chori' as we all call him – to ask for the phone number of his fellow countryman, Godín. Diego Godín has been a central defender for Atlético since 2010. He, too, had just played in the World Cup, scoring the goal against Italy which took his team into the round of 16. A hell of a player who really knows how to head the ball: it was in this manner that before the World Cup he had scored the goal which won Atlético their tenth Spanish Championship in the last game of the Liga season at the Camp Nou, as well as opening the scoring against Real Madrid in the Champions League final. Chori sent me his number, and I called Godín.

"Diego, it's Antoine. You okay?! Tell me, I wanted to know a little about what the dressing room is like, how the coach is and the club..."

"I'm fine, Antoine, and you? Don't worry, it's a very cool dressing room here. We're like a family, really. We're together and we pull together all year round. What's more, the fans are brilliant with us. The club is very ambitious and aims to get to the top. Come, don't be a dick! Go on, come..." He finished by bursting into laughter, saying: "I don't know if we are going to win but we're definitely going to have a laugh!"

After this conversation and Godín's reassuring words, I no longer had any hesitation. Two hours later Éric got things going again. He wanted to know when I was coming home from Turkey, because the Atlético officials were ready to meet me in a restaurant in Lyon. I was already thinking about wearing the club's shirt. I began to become aware of the fact that this certainly wouldn't go down well with the Real Sociedad fans, considering their rivalry with Atlético, but I wanted to go there. I just asked them to respect my decision. But we weren't there yet.

My dad came with me to the meeting in Lyon. He wouldn't understand everything since the talks were in Spanish, but I thought it wise to have him by my side at that time. Miguel Ángel Gil Marín, who was Atlético's majority shareholder and managing director, Andrea Berta, the sporting director, and other club members, attended the meal. They had made the journey just for me. In other words they were scoring points.

It was during this meeting that my transfer was decided. Miguel Ángel Gil began with the introductions, speaking about the history of the club, its ambitions and what he thought of the team. Naturally I was listening, but the crucial question for me was knowing which position I was going to play in, the style of play, the coach's confidence and the objectives. The length of contract, the salary and the clauses were all secondary for me.

When I insisted he put forward the following argument which struck home: "You know we play 4-4-2 most of the time. We see you as the second striker, alongside Mario Mandžukić. And, from time to time, down the left. How do you feel about playing up front down the middle?"

Ah, there we were! My answer didn't disappoint him. "I used

to play in the middle when I was very young. It's when I became a professional that I was put on the left. But everything will quickly become automatic again after a few training sessions and games."

"Our aim is to fight Barça and Real Madrid for La Liga," Miguel Ángel Gil insisted. "We want to reach the quarter-finals. Then we'll see how far we can go. We would like to have you because we know you are the ideal player in order for us to realise those ambitions."

A second very good point! I glanced over at my dad occasionally. Even if he didn't understand everything because of the language, he listened to every detail. We toasted my transfer when the dessert came. In my mind I was already a *colchonero*, which is the nickname for the players. It means 'mattress maker', referring to the red and white shirt, the colours in which Spanish mattresses were made. I was already identifying myself with Atlético, the club founded in 1903 by Basque students.

My dad and I went over the events on the road back to Mâcon. We were happy. We called my mum, who was also delighted. She was waiting for us at home with a bottle of champagne to celebrate. Erika was thrilled, too. She knew it was important for me to leave so I could continue to progress. And she wouldn't feel too out of place since she was moving nearer one of her closest friends in Madrid. We just had to hope she would settle in well.

That's how I started from scratch, or almost, Atlético having paid my release clause fee. I was able to keep my number seven. I quickly started filling my Atlético trophy cabinet by winning the *Supercopa de España* or the Spanish Supercup against Real Madrid, where I made an assist for Mandžukić. I also scored against Olympiacos in the Champions League and twice in La Liga against Córdoba.

But not everything was going as well as I had envisaged. I had to take on board a new tactic in 4-4-2, with a constant pressing, where I had to put myself in the middle when the game was focused down the right and to go and press when it developed down the left. I had to understand this system, whereas at Real we concentrated less on tactics.

The most puzzling thing was that sometimes I would score and then find myself benched for the next game! I didn't understand. Yet I was giving everything. The coach wasn't talkative. I was also surprised that he would ask me to shoot rather than pass in training.

Diego Godín helped me to feel better in the squad. He made sure I was involved in the barbecues which he organised regularly with the others players, a continuing tradition.

Erika and I moved to the quiet residential area of La Finca, not very far from the training ground. A lot of Atlético and Real Madrid players live there. Among them Cristiano Ronaldo, Gareth Bale, Toni Kroos, my coach and even the club's major shareholder! It's made up of a hundred or so private apartments, all ultra-secure. That's really why we chose it. I didn't want to be worried, when I went away the night before games or anything, about being burgled. I had to protect Erika and Mia from intruders.

Our house in La Finca means we can keep our private life. Once I'm in my sanctuary I rarely go out, except to walk my dog, Hooki, a French bulldog, in the big park. I like his big ears and his snout! I am very much a stay at home person, even more so since my daughter was born. Apart from some trips to a restaurant and to the cinema, I take it easy at home.

I was happy on the pitch, and I enjoyed training. But it didn't stop me from mulling things over when I got back home. I was even disgusted at times. I just didn't follow the coach's logic. I said to Erika: "I don't understand. He's not happy with me and yet I'm trying to do the right thing."

For example, one October, we played host to Juventus at the Vicente Calderón in a Champions League group match. Throughout the week I had been part of the regular team in training. The day before the game, Simeone didn't reveal the 11 who were going to play. During the video session the next morning, on match day, there was still no side announced. I felt I wouldn't be starting.

When we reached the dressing room I realised that my intuition had been correct. I exchanged a few words before kick-off with Juve's two French players, Paul Pogba and 'Uncle Pat', Patrice Evra. I opened up to them about my situation: "It's hard, because I'd been in the team all week." They encouraged me to keep going. "Hang on. Don't worry. You've got what it takes to establish yourself."

I came on in the 53rd minute that night. That's what had been decided by Simeone, who is an awesome figure in Madrid and elsewhere. As a player he was a complete defensive midfielder, ever willing, who made 106 appearances for Argentina. He played in three World Cups and I'm not even angry with him for having got my idol David Beckham sent off in the 1998 tournament! He won three Championships with Inter Milan and Lazio.

When he became a coach at 36, he first worked at home in Argentina and then in 2011 he was named boss of Atlético Madrid, a club he knew off by heart for having been one of the main protagonists of the League and Cup Double in 1996.

Only way is up: In front of a passionate Marseille public, *Les Bleus* knock Germany out of the Euro 2016 semi-finals. I scored both goals in the game and I'm celebrating with my great friend, Paul Pogba

Catch me if you can: In May 2016 I outstrip Cristiano Ronaldo in the Champions League final. But, sadly, Real Madrid beat Atlético Madrid 5-3 on penalties after the game had finished 1-1. One month later Ronaldo wins again in the Euro finals as Portugal beat France 1-0 in extra-time

Tough moment: We were losing 1-0 in the Champions League final to Real Madrid in 2016 when we were awarded a penalty early in the second half – but my spot-kick hit the bar

Comeback kings: At half-time we were 1-0 down but I managed to score two goals to give us a 2-1 win against the Republic of Ireland in the last 16 of Euro 2016

Looking up to the boss: I owe Didier Deschamps so much. *(Right)* Celebrating a goal against Albania with my team-mates during the group stage of Euro 2016

Not this time: I had to settle for a runners-up medal after we lost 1-0 to Portugal in the final of Euro 2016

United we stand: With Lassana Diarra, Patrice Evra, England's Eric Dier, Yohan Cabaye and Bacary Sagna during the friendly with England at Wembley after the Paris terror attacks in 2015

Life isn't just about football: I'm a basketball fan and I've got a court at home. Here I am with my wife Erika at Madison Square Garden, where I went to see the New York Knicks play

Team Grizi: Celebrating with my father after defeating Olympique Marseille in the UEFA Europa League final at the Parc Olympique Lyonnais stadium in 2018

El Cholo: Diego Simeone has shown his faith in me

Double delight: I scored two and was Man of the Match in the UEFA Europa League final

Hitting the spot: *(Top)* Converting my penalty kick in the 38th minute of the 2018 World Cup final to put us back in the lead after Croatia's equaliser. *Above and right:* Celebrating with Raphaël Varane

Ecstasy: Collapsing to my knees as the referee blows his whistle ... we are world champions

Star man: Celebrating with Paul Pogba and Kylian Mbappé after the final in Moscow

Super feeling: Lifting the UEFA Super Cup in August, 2018, after we had beaten our rivals and UEFA Champions League winners Real Madrid 4-2 after extra time in Tallinn

He's a passionate man, who lives for his job. But even if you see him agitated a lot on the bench, he doesn't speak much to me. And never have I asked a coach for explanations; Éric Olhats taught me not to complain. So I would just comply and stay on the bench when he put me there, ready to come on and make the differerence.

I wasn't used to being a substitute. I had to get to grips with my new world, playing for the reigning champions, living up to fans' high expectations. It was clear that I no longer had the same status as at Real Sociedad. Of course, I knew that, but I couldn't wait to be able to show what I could do. I had the opportunity to do that in Bilbao, through Mario Mandžukić's suspension, and I didn't pass it up.

For the sixth match of La Liga, 46,500 people were in the San Mames stands cheering their team on. I drank in the atmosphere. The 46th, 73rd and the 81st: these are the minutes in which I scored. It was a pivotal game. Already, a few weeks earlier against Celta Vigo, when the coach brought me off just after the hour mark, I had felt the public grumble, as if they didn't agree with Simeone's decision. That comforted me: it showed I was on the right track. But the real turning point was Bilbao. I hadn't scored hat-tricks often; I can only remember one other with Real Sociedad. Why that night in particular? I don't know. I hadn't changed my way of playing, nor my attitude on the field. But things went more my way. I was never out of the team again. Feeling you are a regular, someone who is important to the team, is paramount.

Those three goals – as many as I had scored in my first 15 league games – came the day before the holidays. Before leaving, the fitness coach, Oscar Ortega, had asked me to be careful during the festive period and not to return with a few too many kilos. It was a message which meant: you've just won your place, so don't go spoiling it all. I was beginning to take in what the coach was asking of me, to become more clinical up front and to work harder, mainly on the defensive side. At Real Sociedad I didn't track back a lot.

Ortega's work was paying off. The man we call 'The Teacher' is an essential part of Atlético's success. This Uruguayan has worked with Diego Simeone since the start of his coaching career. It's thanks to him that injuries are rare at the club. Our physical condition is excellent. He warms us up for ten to 15 minutes before each game in order to avoid any muscle trouble. He is always fussing over us.

His pre-season work is frightening. It takes place 40 minutes outside Madrid, in Los Angeles de San Rafael, and lasts for about two weeks. On the first day back we do a lot of running, climbing hills on the golf courses. I've already seen some of the club's young players throw their guts up. But, thanks to these intense efforts, we are in form for the whole season, continuing to press strongly up front and at the back for 90 minutes. I started after the others when I signed because I had benefited from a few extra days of recovery due to the World Cup. The Teacher made me run a lot, which is something I didn't do much at Real Sociedad. Nothing is left to chance and the players' body mass index is checked every morning. Since I've been in Madrid, I haven't exceeded my playing weight, which is 72 kilos (11.3 stone).

From the moment of that hat-trick in Bilbao, I forgot the difficulties I'd experienced in familiarising myself with this intense physical preparation, the style of play and the constant demands. From then on everything fell into place naturally. The proof: I finished my first season at Atlético

Madrid with 25 goals, 22 of which came in the league, my highest total. Third in the championship and knocked out of the Champions League quarter-final by Real Madrid, I had played 53 games and claimed my first trophy with the club, the Spanish Supercup.

Simeone had been right not to lose faith in me. When people were questioning my inefficiency at the start of the season, *El Cholo* had been clear in the press conference, assuring me that I was "a much more complete player than a simple winger." He also said: "The closer he gets to goal the more he will explode as a footballer. He is going to have to work for a while so he can exploit all his attributes: the changes of direction, short diagonal runs, working between the lines, his back-to-goal game and his good mid-range shot. We hope the important youngster, which he is, will start to become a man and a player who is equally important."

He was right. I learn from him every day and I want to carry on doing that. He is also very good tactically, for example on set-pieces. He doesn't speak a lot to the players but when he's got something to say he says it to your face, either by taking you to one side or in front of the squad. His massive confidence rubs off on the players. He's not going to leave them out if they haven't scored for a game or two. He is so intensely involved in the matches that he can be scary if you don't know him. But this way of being at one with us pushes us further and gives us an extra determination.

It's thanks to Simeone that I became the player I am. Our trust in each other is reciprocal. Always dressed in black during the games, he has an undeniable charisma. He exudes something special. The players and the fans respect him enormously. They all know what they owe him. He put Atlético Madrid back on the scene. He never speaks to us about his playing career and, even though he stays switched on he doesn't get involved in training except, now and again, to send over crosses when we're working on heading at goal. We talk about the team, but when it comes to signings I would never allow myself to suggest such and such a player to him. That's not my style.

There is another essential Diego: Godín. We are great mates. He was brilliant with me right from the start. We always sit next to each other when we're on the move, and our wives get on well, too. Apart from Diego, my other closest friends during early days at Atlético were Nicolás Gaitán *(2)*, Ángel Correa and José Maria Giménez. That's the maté gang! Atlético is a real family club. It's a calm dressing room, as was so at Real Sociedad. I was surprised at first because the club had just been crowned champions and had reached the Champions League final. There are no cliques and there's a cheery atmosphere. And everyone makes an effort when a new guy arrives.

Our journey through the group phase of the 2015/2016 Champions League had been tricky. Basically we made hard work of it! We'd started well enough with a victory in Istanbul against Galatasaray (2-0). I scored both goals in under ten minutes. But a fortnight later we lost at home to Benfica. We got a 4-0 win against Astana then a 0-0 in Kazakhstan before beating Galatasaray again (2-0). And again I scored both goals, one with a header and then with a side-foot. I received an ovation when I came off. To top the group we needed to win in Portugal, which we did against Benfica.

So we're in the round of 16, facing PSV Eindhoven. It was a tight and tense confrontation. In the first leg we returned from Holland with a solid 0-0 draw. I could even have scored. But, following a forward pass, I failed in my one-on-one with their keeper. I wanted to dink the ball, except that I was wearing iron studs and the boot didn't slip under the leather of the ball enough.

Despite our numerous goal attempts in the second leg, we were unable to make the breakthrough. After extra-time the tie would be decided on penalties. I scored from our first one with an angled shot, and we ran out 8-7 winners. It was never ending. The first failure only came on the 15th attempt, when the ball struck the bar! Then Juanfran converted his kick, which sent us through into the quarter-finals.

Atlético were also on a good run in the league. For example, in the Santiago Bernabéu, we had inflicted on Real Madrid their first defeat since Zinedine Zidane had become their coach. I scored the game's only goal from a pass from Filipe Luis.

Next up was Barcelona in the Champions League. A brace from Luis Suarez meant we went down (2-1) in the Camp Nou. It was a strange game because Fernando Torres had opened the scoring for us before being sent off for a second yellow card before half-time. It meant we had to play with ten men for an hour.

Barça kept pushing for a third goal to give them a cushion, which meant that their players were afraid. I was certain we were still alive in the tie. I knew that, with our fans behind us and our excellent physical condition, we were capable of causing an upset and eliminating the holders. The pitch was dry at Calderón; that's how you need it to be when you're up against Barcelona because if the surface is wet the ball moves too quickly! It was the perfect scenario.

First I scored with a good header from Saul Niguez's pass

with the outside of his boot, and I wasn't offside because Dani Alves was playing me on. This was the opportunity to acknowledge my progress and prove that I was becoming a real fox in the box. I jumped very high to make that header.

Then, at the end of the game, I got my second with a penalty, awarded after a handball by Iniesta. I scuffed my shot a little, but it went in. They were already my 28th and 29th goals of the season. It was a magical night right till the end because the coach took me off shortly after the penalty and I was warmly applauded!

With Barça floored, it meant there was one favourite fewer in the race. We were waiting to find out our next opponents. We had the feeling that we'd get Real Madrid, which didn't exactly thrill us. We were in training when we heard that the draw had paired us with Bayern Munich. Another big gun! Their team was coached by Pep Guardiola, which meant that they were going to move the ball, like at Barcelona, where he laid the foundations of the game.

We won the first leg 1-0, thanks to a great goal by Saul Niguez, who ended his slalom with a curled left foot shot. As in the previous round we played on a dry surface. The fans pushed us all the way so we could keep the lead, which came in the 11th minute. We defended as if our lives depended on it. Our play isn't always pleasant but it's very effective.

The return match was epic. Xabi Alonso equalised on aggregate with a deflected free-kick. Bayern were awarded a penalty, just three minutes later, in the 34th minute. Thomas Müller took it but Jan Oblak saved his shot as well as Xabi Alonso's follow-up attempt. That was without doubt the turning point of the game. If they had gone 2-0 ahead we would probably have lost. Bayern played a fantastic first half, their best of the Guardiola era. They were so on top, while we were all over the place.

The coach said the right things in the dressing room. He asked us to give it our all, not to let in another goal and he guaranteed we would score. And if that were to be the case, Atlético would go through. He gave us belief. We started the second half on the front foot. On a counter-attack in the 54th minute I got the ball near the centre circle, I headed it to Fernando Torres, who played it forwards into my path. I went like a rocket, beating the offside trap, and I headed straight towards Manuel Neuer's goal.

On this one-on-one I made him think I was going to open my body, but at the last moment I dropped my shoulder and fired a straight low shot. The ball ended up in the corner of the net. Atlético were virtually in the final. We just had to hold out. That was no easy matter.

Robert Lewandowski regained Bayern's lead in the 74th minute. We were still going through, but another goal meant the Bavarians would knock us out. I gave way eight minutes later, while in the 84th minute Fernando Torres won a penalty after a foul by Javi Martínez. If he scored it was all over. Unfortunately Manuel Neuer fisted the ball away. At that point, I admit, I was afraid. They were superior. Atlético put in a crazy performance. I've spoken about this with the players: it's the match in which we suffered the most under Diego Simeone. I'd even asked to come off. We were dominated and we needed someone fresher. Bayern were attacking down the flanks, someone had to block them and I was no longer able to defend.

Incidentally, and this didn't come out at the time, I may not even have played in this semi-final, second leg. I'd had a muscular problem for quite a while. A lump behind my hamstring was bothering me. I didn't say anything to the coach. I only opened up about it to Jesús Vázquez, the club's physiotherapist, who replied: "Don't worry. We're going to work hard and you'll be able to play." We did work, but I didn't feel confident.

On the morning of the game, I even thought about telling the coach that I was in too much pain. I was suffering even when I walked. I took some anti-inflammatories and I held firm. I offered Jesús my shirt. He deserved it because he took care of me, and it's thanks to him that I was able to score.

We were at the crossroads of our ambitions because we were also competing for La Liga, level on points with Barcelona. But our illusions were shattered in the penultimate match against Levante.

I came on at half-time when the score was 1-1 and they scored near the end. On the night of the 38th and final championship match, a win against Celta Vigo where I opened the scoring, could only leave us in third place, three points behind Barça and two behind Real Madrid. Our season was going to hinge on the Champions League final, against Real, in Milan.

I will always have mixed feelings about May 28th, 2016, in the San Siro.

There were more than 70,000 fans, but I wasn't impressed with the atmosphere. I was pleased to see so many people in the stadium even though, when our bus arrived near the ground and when I was listening to music, I was picked out by some Real fans who hurled bottles which smashed the window. A few metres further on we passed in front of the Atlético fans, who encouraged us, tapping the bus as a way of saying 'good luck'.

The match seemed fairly balanced. Real scored first after a quarter of an hour through Sergio Ramos from a Toni Kroos free-kick. We were going to have to do more running. But I believed in us, I felt good. I positioned myself behind Casemiro, between the Brazilian defensive midfielder and the central defenders, so I could hurt them, create danger and try to get shots in. The coach was also confident at half-time. "I feel we're going to win and level the score," he told us.

The second half had barely begun when we won a penalty after Fernando Torres had been fouled by Pepe from my pass. Between the time when Mark Clattenburg blew and the walk to the penalty spot to take my kick, I only had one idea in mind: 'Shoot in the middle and it will go in.' I didn't change my mind. And my shot rebounded off the crossbar.

I was sad, pissed off. Loads of bad things had happened in the space of a minute. Mentally we had to get ourselves motivated again and try to forget about it. I won back as many balls as possible straight away in order to get my confidence back.

Fortunately, in the 79th minute, Yannick Carrasco, who had come on at half-time, equalised. It was such a relief for me because I was blaming myself. And I still blame myself today. I think that if I had equalised, as expected, we would have won the game.

There was no winner at the end of normal time, so we headed into two 15 minute periods of extra-time, then into a penalty shoot-out. I didn't hesitate for a second: I wanted to be the first one to go. "If you miss," I said to myself, "your team-mates will have four other chances to right your mistake." I hoped that our superkeeper, Jan Oblak, would save one.

On my turn, I waited for Keylor Navas to dive one way and I opened my body to shoot in the other direction. I yelled after my goal, partly because I was relieved and partly to hammer to myself: "You should have done that before!" But because I'd decided to go down the middle ... Juanfran, our fourth taker, shot against the post and Cristiano Ronaldo sealed the win for Real Madrid, five penalties to three.

No-one had a go at me in the dressing room about my missed penalty. I am not ashamed to say that I cried. We had knocked out the champions of Holland, Spain and Germany, only to fall so close to home. We just lacked that bit of luck which would have allowed us to lift the trophy. In the event of a win, I had planned a party at home with my mates. Obviously I cancelled it all.

I didn't have too much time to dwell on my disappointment because, two days afterwards, I was joining up with the France team. The Euros helped me to move on, even if I thought about it for the next few nights. That said, it was all forgotten about, after the opening game of the tournament against Romania.

I began my third season at Atlético Madrid with gusto. The proof: I was named Player of the Month in La Liga for September 2016, with five goals and an assist in four matches. We were top of the league at the time. I scored in the next game against Valencia but then went ten matches without a goal. Things got back on track after a life-saving break with the family during the Christmas period. Actually, I often suffer a dip in form in November/December due to fatigue and stress. By mid-March, 2017, I had totted up 14 goals in 27 League games.

Atlético didn't win the title but our objective was to grab fourth place, which qualifies us for the Champions League. We did better than that, finishing third behind Barcelona and the eventual champions Real Madrid.

In the Champions League, we were top of Group D, ahead of Bayern Munich, and we eliminated Bayern Leverkusen in the round of 16. We had reached the club's fourth consecutive quarter-final.

Before the last eight game against Leicester City *(3)* I had registered four goals that season. By scoring one in Germany against Bayer on February 21st 2017, I became the top scorer in European competition in Atlético's history, with 13 goals in 29 games. I broke the record which Luis Aragonés set in 1974, 43 years earlier.

Aragonés is a legend in Madrid: a striker who played for a decade at Atlético, winning three league titles and two Cups, before coaching the club for over ten years, when he won one La Liga, three King's Cups, one Super Cup and one Intercontinental Cup. As coach of Spain, he helped them become European Champions in 2008. From now on, I, too, am part of the history of the club and I'm proud of it.

(1) In March 2017 Le Journal de Mickey, a weekly French comic magazine, compiled a list of the 50 favourite personalities among 7-14 year-olds. The poll places Antoine Griezmann in second place behind the French rapper Soprano.

(2) Nicolás Gaitán and Yannick Carrasco joined Chinese Super League team Dalian Yifang in February 2018. Dalian Yifang are owned by Atlético Madrid part-owners Wanda Group.

(3) Atlético Madrid beat Leicester City 1-0 in the first leg of the Champions League final at Vicente Calderón.

Antoine Griezmann scored the winning goal in the 28th minute from the penalty spot. A 1-1 draw at the King Power Stadium in the return leg saw Atlético through to a semi-final against city rivals Real Madrid. Another Griezmann penalty helped Atlético to a 2-1 win in the home leg but a Cristiano Ronaldo hat-trick in a 3-0 win at the Santiago Bernabéu Stadium saw Real through to the final which was held at the Millennium Stadium in Cardiff. Real beat Juventus 4-1 to claim their 12th European Cup.

17

TEAMWORK AND THE KILLER INSTINCT

According to the literature, I'm 1.75 metres (5'7½") or 1.76 meters (5'8") tall. Where does the truth lie? I don't know. Let's say somewhere in between. My height has never been a handicap, even though it turned out to be a hindrance for scouts when I was chasing trials in France. Everything changed and was forgotten as soon as I arrived in Spain.

At Real Sociedad I no longer heard "you're the small one" but the following question, which was clearly more pertinent: "Are you good or not?" I was physically behind the others but I knew I was going to grow, even if it was clear that I would never reach two metres (6'5").

I don't match the pre-conceived ideas of a modern footballer, someone who is taller and more athletic than me. But I make up for that in other ways. Certainly, when you run up to take a penalty against Manuel Neuer and his 1.93 metre (6'3") arm span, it makes an impression on you.

Nevertheless tall players have never been a particular problem for me. Of course, I prefer not to face a central defender as strapping as Sergio Ramos. This type of player sticks to you everywhere and is hard to shake off. I cope with it. Against this kind of opponent, even more than usual, I take one or two touches of the ball, I lead him to the right and to the left so as to take advantage of a reaction time which inevitably at some time or other won't be as quick. It's hard for the tall players to track the smaller ones! It's rare for Lionel Messi to be stopped.

I'm not a mountain of muscles and I never work out; I don't like it. However, I am determined to get the better of people with my legs, through my speed with the ball, guile and by dodging. I am all about avoiding opponents. I have learned to be smart, especially in the box. I hate taking knocks and coming into contact. It seems to work: my injuries are light. I'm not a player who dribbles and keeps hold of the ball. I understood very quickly that the centimetres which I lacked in height I had to make up for in speed.

I have to be a killer in the box, even though I love being a team player. It's up to me to make both aspects work together. Diego Simeone, my coach, wants me to score, to get close to the goal.

In other words, to be a fox in the box. I loved AC Milan's Filippo Inzaghi when I was young. I used to watch his games. You often wouldn't see him during the match but he would end up scoring two not very attractive goals. Some people don't consider him to be a great player, but every coach would dream of having a Pippo Inzaghi in his team.

The coach doesn't really appreciate it when I drop back to get the ball. But I've liked to pass the ball ever since I was small and I continue to do so. Initially it was hard at Atlético because I was supposed to score goals even though I didn't see myself as an out-and-out number nine. I am not obsessed about scoring.

The proof is that in general I only shoot no more than twice in a game. I didn't even muster one shot when I was with *Les Bleus* against Holland in Amsterdam. I didn't see any opportunity to do so in the game. That can seem frustrating but the main thing is to win, which we did thanks to a sweet strike from Paul Pogba.

I should shoot more but I do what my head tells me. I don't go looking for an individual opportunity at all costs. And I rarely shoot from distance, even though it can happen depending on how inspired I feel, as illustrated by a powerful first time left foot drive at La Coruña for the equaliser, after I'd seen the keeper off his line.

Usually I shoot from inside the box, and I just do what's required. Never any frills. From memory I have never had more than five attempts at goal in one game. The five were against Deportivo Alavés. Five failures. It was the first time I'd failed to score with as many shots.

I know very well that I'll be judged on the number of goals. If I score, then good, but it's not my main objective. I get the same pleasure when I make an assist for others to find the net. I can go thirty minutes up front without touching the ball. If I see that the team needs me to be more available, I'll drop a bit, even if the coach won't like it.

All I'm interested in is being able to hurt the defence and create a chance. I want to feel good on the field, so leave me alone. You want me to defend? No problem, just as long as I'm allowed to do what I want up front.

I take pride in the fact that I'm a complete player, both in defensive and attacking terms. I tackle a lot, which is something of a rarity for strikers. The number of goals I scored in the last Euros is what will immediately spring to mind, because a goalscorer is under the spotlight. But, once again, I don't focus on that. That's not how I am, and there is much more to my game.

Later on, I would like people to remember me as a complete striker, who knew how to do it all, and who was a team player as well as a goalscorer. I know statistics are important in football. I should be more selfish sometimes. But that's not my mindset. I never hesitate to point out the work of Koke or previously Gabi (our former captain). They receive less media coverage, and they are spoken about less, but they're the ones who make the team win. I pick them out insomuch as it goes with my philosophy. It is also a way of letting them know what I think of them, that I know what we owe them and that they must continue to sacrifice themselves for us. In any case, everyone defends at Atlético. A player can win you a game but not a competition.

My strength is in my anticipation. When I'm given the ball I know where my team-mates are. I analyse things in front of me so as to find the best way of surprising the defender. To hurt him I can move out wide or put myself behind the number six and call for the ball to be played forwards. I am mindful of where the ball's going to land or where the cross will end up, if I have to move in front of the defender or wait at the far post. The important thing is always being in the place where the ball will drop.

I also use videos which the club makes available to us. The coach shows us them on the days before matches. After the games I receive an e-mail of my combined activity. This work helps me when I'm analysing situations, the reality of which I can only partially appreciate when I'm on the field.

I am focused in the extreme during training. I do everything thoroughly. I see an opportunity to try things and to fine-tune how I spin around and attack. When I'm lacking confidence and there's a big match coming up I double my effort. I stay behind after training with the third-choice goalkeeper and take part in a shooting session. I connect with the powerful low crosses which are sent over to me.

I add a bit of spice by making bets, setting myself challenges. I promise, for example, that I'll put at least three of the next five shots away. Or I'll bet on a series of penalties. If the keeper stops one I give him a bottle of wine. So far I haven't had to pay out! It's a moment of relaxation but also a healthy form of stress, with a shot of adrenaline. I need competition and to have contact with the ball.

Before, when I received it, I would give it back straight away, even when no-one was challenging me. I now endeavour to turn around so I can set up moves and create danger. *El Cholo* has taught me a lot. Re-deployed in the middle, the winger which I was brought up as has had to evolve. From now on I'm confident and I'm trying new things.

This effectiveness is also fine-tuned in my recovery and healthy lifestyle. I know my body, I know when I need to rest and sleep. I watch what I eat, even though I sometimes dream of a McDonald's and occasionally I'm gagging for a burger! I don't eat to excess. I keep my fluids up and I drink lots of water. At home I've recently employed someone who cooks for us, so

I can eat a more balanced diet while at the same time relieving Erika, who is wrapped up with Mia.

However, despite everything, I still love my food. A good steak hachè for example, or my mum's tartiflette *(1)*. The further away the game is the more I can let myself go. I alter my intake as and when the match approaches. Atlético Madrid weigh us every day and pay a particular attention to our body mass index. Mine doesn't change. When several players are above their correct weight the fitness coach sends a warning to each of them. I can guarantee you it's quite a deterrent…

(1) A dish from Savoy Alps in south-eastern France. It is made with potatoes, Reblochon cheese, lardons and onions.

18

GOLDEN VISION

I couldn't help but apologise. The final of the Euros had barely finished and the wound was still fresh. When I went to collect the Golden Boot, the trophy awarded to the competition's top scorer, I caught the gaze of Didier Deschamps on the stairs leading to the official gallery. "I'm really sorry I didn't score," I told the coach, my voice trembling. "But I gave everything. That's it, I'm really sorry."

The words just came out spontaneously. He immediately eased my frustration. "You don't have to be sorry, you had a great tournament. It's no big deal..."

Of course I was happy to receive an award from UEFA. But the pride would come later. At the time I was devastated, as were all my team-mates. I was disappointed not to have found a way through against Portugal and not to have managed to score so that we could triumph collectively. I hate to think of myself in individual terms. I get infuriated by people who behave in such a way, on the field and in the dressing room. My first consideration is for the squad. My immediate thoughts were about the older players, who were no doubt playing their last international tournament in 2016. The outcome was cruel.

But I prefer to harbour happy memories, such as the second half against the Republic of Ireland in the round of 16, which changed everything. *Les Bleus* were taken to Lyon, 70 kilometres from my house in Mâcon. In the first half, I had been played out wide, in the 4-3-3 formation which the coach favoured. At half-time we were 1-0 down to a second minute Robbie Brady penalty.

The atmosphere in the dressing room was electric. Hugo Lloris, Steve Mandanda, Patrice Evra, in short the 'leaders' who are accustomed to expressing themselves, did the talking. "Hey, lads, with all respect to our opponents, we can't get knocked out by Ireland. It can't happen. What's more, not at home. Now, let's wake up and move our arses!"

Deschamps said: "We're going to 4-2-3-1 with Antoine down the middle." I said to myself that that was good. It was up to me to play and make this my half. Sure, 45 minutes can seem a short time in which to make the difference, but I felt this was the right moment to come to the fore. This is what I had been waiting for. I had hoped to be given the nod to play higher up the field like at Atlético Madrid.

I moved to the middle when I got back on the pitch with Olivier Giroud, whom I could play off, and with Dimitri Payet and Kingsley Coman – who replaced N'Golo Kanté – in support. It was up to me to take responsibility. I was convinced this tactical switch would allow me to be the player I was aspiring to be. I was feeling confident, my Champions League goals against Barcelona and Bayern Munich having proved to me that I had what it takes. It was now just a matter of repeating it against the Republic of Ireland…

With fire in our bellies, we began the second half much better. We put together a great move from the start, which increased our desire tenfold. The supporters got behind us, seeing that we were hungry.

In the 58th minute Bacary Sagna delivered a good cross to me from the right towards the penalty spot. I rose to meet it with my head. You've got to connect powerfully in this situation otherwise the goalkeeper will make the save. It was on my good side, the timing was impeccable and I gave it all I had. It was a header across goal which Darren Randolph touched but couldn't keep out. It was just as well I'd got some force into it. The equaliser boosted us. I didn't really know how to celebrate my goal, so I made for the bench!

Three minutes later, from Laurent Koscielny's long pass, Olivier Giroud, who was battling with two defenders on the flank, headed the ball perfectly into my path. Put through on goal I got into the Irish box and scored with a left foot shot across their keeper. We had turned things around in just 180 seconds. On my second goal Dimitri Payet got hold of my left foot and pretended to kiss it. I celebrated it with a nod to Drake, shaking both hands with my thumbs and little fingers extended, like the rapper in his 'Hotline Bling' video. I had already planned this, but I forgot against Albania because the emotion got the better of me.

It may sound pretentious but, as a matter of fact, it's true: I'd been convinced that I'd score if I was played in this position. My club coaches and those in the national teams were advocating the same. Olivier's work had been vital on the second goal. He attracts the ball and the defenders with his tall frame, so much so that it makes space for me. He is a precious outlet, who can play as a target man, and I always look for him as he can give me a return pass with one touch of the ball. At 2-1 up there was no way we were going to lose. In addition, in the 66th minute I brought about the sending off of Shane Duffy, who tackled me late. I twice came close towards the end to scoring a hat-trick from Dimitri's crosses. Still, I became the first France player to net three goals in the Euros since Zidane in 2004.

After the game, I gave the ball to the son of the police commander who had been murdered a few days earlier in Maganville *(1)*. I also gave him the match ball, which was signed by all the players. It seemed normal to do something nice for him. We've got the power to give people a dream, so why not use it? Sometimes people make ill-considered judgements about footballers. But we are not disconnected. I am aware that a smile, a gesture or a photo are courtesies which can mean a lot to our fans. Besides, young Hugo was going through a terrible ordeal.

My Euros took off after Ireland. As the coach is sometimes stubborn, I'd been afraid that he would revert to a 4-3-3 for the quarter-final. In fact, he joked about that all week in training and we laughed about it together. That was the start of a closer relationship. I was able to speak to him more freely as well as to his faithful number two, Guy Stephan. From then on there's no doubt I felt I had more right to do so.

In our minds, we were going to play England in the quarter-final at the Stade de France. But Iceland beat them to everyone's surprise. I was happy to avoid the English, whom I thought would be hard to beat and very motivated when up against our players who performed in their league. So it would be Iceland, a country of 330,000 people and 20,000 registered footballers, who were taking part in their first big international tournament, with most of their players operating in Sweden or Denmark. Even though we were massive favourites, this wasn't going to be a formality. There is character in this volcanic island and it was not to be taken lightly: its team had twice beaten Holland in the Euro qualifiers. In the first round it had held Portugal and Hungary to a draw and had beaten Austria, before going on to knock England out.

We studied the Icelandic style and their long ball game at length, notably their throw-ins, which seemed like corners. But that Sunday, July 3rd, went like a dream. I was again picked to play down the middle and we quickly got stuck into the task. Everything went smoothly. We were already 4-0 up at half-time!

Olivier Giroud had opened the scoring and Paul Pogba put us further ahead with a header from one of my corners. In the 43rd minute I made an assist for Dimitri Payet to score our third. Two minutes later it was my turn to get in on the act: Paul made the opening, Olivier touches it to me and I home in on the keeper who I surprise with a left foot dink. I went over to the bench to share my joy. The others said to me: "I knew you were going to do that..." It's true that, when there's no keeper in goal during a training exercise, I like to dink the ball.

I celebrated my goal by sliding on the turf, then by pretending to drink from a baby's bottle, as a way of dedicating it to my daughter. We dealt with things in the second half, Olivier scoring another goal, while the Icelanders beat Hugo Lloris twice.

We had to put this out of our minds four days later in the Vélodrome in Marseille, against World Champions Germany, who had happened to knock us out of the quarter-finals of the Brazil World Cup. While *Les Bleus* had beaten Germany to third place in the 1958 World Cup, they had always got the better of us since in a major tournament. I wasn't harbouring a feeling of revenge with regard to history. We just wanted, on that July 7th, to get to the final and face Portugal, who had knocked out Gareth Bale's Wales the day before.

The atmosphere in Marseille was exceptional. I love this stadium, which was the most beautiful one in the Euros. The fervour of the supporters took us to a different level. It was the same starting XI as against Iceland. Once again, I was up front, buzzing around Olivier. What more could I ask for? The warm-up was quality, but the pitch was in a very average state. That was one of the competition's weak points. I carved out a chance with my first touch of the ball: a one-two with Blaise Matuidi and then a right foot shot from just inside the box which the goalkeeper dived low to push away. That was a good sign. I felt confident.

Our tactic was to let the Germans have the ball and to hit them on the counter-attack, and it paid off. In the 45th minute, Bastian Schweinsteiger handled one of my corners when he was challenging Patrice. I was pleasantly surprised that the referee blew! I took the penalty, hitting it high to Manuel Neuer's right. He was wrong-footed, but I hadn't struck the ball particularly well.

When I got hold of the ball to put it on the penalty spot, in my head I was thinking: 'Make amends for the Champions League'. I wasn't afraid to try my luck after my failure against Real Madrid a month earlier. Mentally I needed to have another go. "Open your body, put it high and you'll be fine…" I swore to myself. I chose to side-foot it and it went in; it was a bit of a relief. The stadium was sizzling. In the dressing room it was all about continuing to defend well and not conceding.

We resisted the Germans' pressure while our captain, Hugo Lloris, was imperious. Deliverance came in the 72nd minute when Paul Pogba had a bit of fun before sending over a cross. Neuer came out to knock the ball away with the tip of his gloves, except that I had anticipated things. I waited for the ball to drop and I toe-poked it between his legs to finish off Paul's work. I knew right then that we had to stay solid. 2-0 for *Les Bleus*. I'd had a bit of good fortune but I showed I was opportunistic. The stadium exploded with joy.

The coach withdrew me in stoppage time for Yohan Cabaye so I could reap the applause from the crowd. The communion with the supporters was beautiful. We did the famous thunderclap, like the Icelanders, at the final whistle. Everyone was happy. We were like kids and we didn't want to leave, eager to extend the pleasant taste of victory. The place was really on fire, the fans carried us from start to finish in Marseille, which hadn't been the case everywhere.

With six goals I strengthened my position as the tournament's top scorer, achieving the highest total in a Euro since Michel Platini's nine goals in 1984. Even when we were at Clairefontaine we could feel lots of positive vibes from all the country. We received videos of people in the street proclaiming their love for *Les Bleus*. France was finally feeling good. Now it was a question of finishing the job… After Real Madrid in the San Siro, here I was again in a major European final. Unfortunately I would experience a similar outcome.

I have never watched that final again, nor any part of it. I don't want to, even though it remains rooted in my memory. There were many turning points. The first occurred when we walked onto the pitch. The stadium had remained lit for a large part of the previous night because of the rehearsals for the closing ceremony, so much so that the sky was full of moths, which were flying over the field. There were hundreds and hundreds of insects. It wasn't very pleasant because some of them brushed against our eyes. I wondered if the Portuguese had put a spell on us?! But they didn't bother us once the match was under way.

Next there was the premature withdrawal of their captain, Cristiano Ronaldo, who got injured after a clash with Dimitri Payet. I could have opened the scoring early into the match but my header was spectacularly tipped away by Rui Patricio. I urged the fans to get behind us. Deprived of their best player, the Portuguese held firm. I knew that if we were to score first it would be all over, but so far nothing had gone in.

The half-time talk was one of determination: "We've got to give it our all, lads. There are only 45 minutes to go, so we've got to push." I wanted that too, but I was worn out, dead. My legs had gone, there was no more juice in the tank. Also, I had been followed around, like my own shadow, by the Portuguese rearguard. I couldn't get the ball. Whether I roamed to the left or to the right I always had someone behind me. It made sense, but it didn't make it any less unpleasant. We continued to create danger in the second half. The chances were there, but we weren't being smiled upon.

I thought I was going to make the difference in the 66th minute. From a cross from Kingsley Coman, who had just come on, I beat Raphaël Guerreiro to the ball with my head in the six-yard box. But I positioned myself too far in front of the defender, so I wasn't on my good side. As things turned out, I was a hair's breadth away from winning the game for *Les Bleus*...

And what about the match-winning opportunity in stoppage time, with André-Pierre Gignac's shot which hit the post when the keeper, for once, was beaten? I wasn't far away from that. I could have got the rebound, but I didn't have enough in my legs to stick out my foot and push the ball into the net. I was knackered. 0-0 at the end of normal time. So we had to go to extra-time, and maybe even penalties. I was totally out of it. I couldn't keep up. I gave everything, I took the corners, but I was exhausted. Mentally I was fine but my legs had gone.

Fate had its way in the 109th minute when Eder, who had come on near the end of the game, let fly with a powerful low shot from 25 metres, which Hugo couldn't do anything about.

It was tough, very tough.

Even though there were still 11 minutes left I suspected we wouldn't get over this. Of course, we laid siege to their goal but there was nothing doing. What disillusionment.

Getting to the final was perfect but the most important thing was winning it. When you suffer two setbacks of this kind in six weeks you start asking yourself questions: why me? Am I going to go through this sort of thing again? It all went through my head.

Even though I had cried hard after Germany had eliminated us in the quarter-finals in Brazil, I held firm this time. I had grown up, so I had to set an example. I went to get some of my team-mates' heads up, to show that we were there for them.

Dédé Gignac was crying. Pat Evra wasn't doing well. He was so disappointed. I had never seen him like this before. Didier Deschamps is a winner. As a player, he was a World and European Champion with *Les Bleus* and a winner of the Champions League with Marseille and Juventus. As a coach, he had won a League Cup and reached the Champions

League final with Monaco, plus a Serie B title with Juve, and the league and League Cup with Marseille. This time, unfortunately, he lost, which is rare. Despite having a great run in the tournament, it was hard to find the right words after you've lost a European final at home. We then met up with our families in the hotel. It was good to see the people who are close to us. When Cristiano Ronaldo won the Champions League with Real I didn't watch him lift the trophy. On this occasion I wanted to see him and his team-mates do it, while hoping that at the next Euros, in four years' time, I'd be doing the same thing.

I was voted Player of Euro 2016 the next day by a jury made up of 13 technical observers *(2)*. It was comforting but I wasn't concerned about that. I so wanted *Les Bleus* to win in front of our fans. I was desperate for only one thing after such a gruelling season: to cut myself off. Before that, we had a lunch at the Élysée Palace to honour an invitation from the Head of State. We didn't really have the heart for this type of event, but we were well received. I went to look at the kitchens, to see what it was like there. Well, there are a lot of people in the Élysée kitchens! I asked them how they were all able to manage considering it was hot. It was nice to look at things from the other side.

Francois Hollande's speech was warm, but I'd have preferred it if we had brought him the Cup. The President of the Republic had visited us at Clairefontaine, where he spent time with Paul Pogba, Patrice Evra, Hugo Lloris and me. He has criticised footballers in a book *(3)* but in making a trip to our centre he would recognise that we are good blokes, well educated and with our heads firmly on our shoulders. Everyone is free to have their opinions.

Right, now time for holidays. I put the phone away and I left for Corsica with my family. I took things easy. Most of all I didn't want to do anything. I wanted to cut myself off totally. I also went to Los Angeles, Miami and Las Vegas, where I was able to take in a basketball match between the United States and Argentina, which was a qualifier for the Rio Olympics. I was finally starting to make the most of the holidays. I tried not to think about football.

Before the Euros I still felt something of a newcomer, whereas today I am perceived as an important player in the eyes of my team-mates and the coach. That's the main thing. That doesn't make me one of the 'leaders'. For example, I don't go around giving tactical advice to the people who burst onto the scene. I'm not looking for people to connect with me at all costs or to show that I'm cool, but if I see that a player on the field had different options available, then I don't hesitate to tell him. I'm not one of the bosses in the France team. That doesn't go with my character.

A lot of people wonder who is in charge in the dressing room. There is no boss and I'm not sure we even need one. All the players are free to have their say. What matters to me is the togetherness. If, rather than scoring, I can help someone else find the net, then I'll never hesitate to do so. That's my strong point. I aspire to be a complete player.

I still have time to become, why not, the captain of *Les Bleus*. I wouldn't be against it, if the coach decided, but I'm not pushing for it. I was captain of the Under-13s in Mâcon with my dad and for one or two games at junior level at Real Sociedad *(4)*. I'm not going to be a better player just by having that bit of material on my arm. Anyway, it's rare for me to speak in the dressing room when I'm with *Les Bleus* and in any case, Didier Deschamps remains the boss. He put his trust in me by giving me my first appearance and it has never wavered since *(5)*. I know what I owe him. I'm ready to fight for him all the time.

(1) The officer had been stabbed to death several times while on his way home to the Yvelines. The assailant, who claimed responsibility for the Islamic State group, was shot dead by officers of the RAID (Recherche, Assistance, Intervention, Dissuasion, an elite tactical unit of the French National Police) who had been deployed there. The victim's wife, a civil servant in the Home Office, was found dead. One of their sons was invited by the Home Secretary to the France-Ireland game and watched Les Bleus train at Clairefontaine.

(2) UEFA's Technical Director, the Romanian Ioan Lupescu, who headed the voting panel, declaired: "Antoine Griezmann was a danger in every game he played. He worked hard for his team. He is a skilful player with good vision and very good finishing ability. The technical observers unanimously decided that he sailed through the tournament."

(3) "Un president ne devrait pas dire ça…" ("Not what a president should say…") by Gérard Davet and Fabrice Lhomme, Stock, 2016.

(4) Griezmann was named as one of four captains of Atlético Madrid in August 2018 alongside Diego Godín (primary captain), Koke and Juanfran.

(5) Asked in a press conference about Griezmann's role in the national team, Deschamps said in October 2016: "Antoine is a leader of the attack. He lives and breathes football, he smiles and he gets the others training. I'm not going to ask him to make speeches or to rally the troops. That's not him and he doesn't want to."

19

KING OF THE WORLD

"Ballon d'Or or no Ballon d'Or. Right now I don't really care about that. I just want to win the World Cup and so we've got to give everything on the field to make that happen."

Two years earlier, Antoine Griezmann had suffered the double heartbreak of losing a Champions League final and a European Championship final, so falling at the ultimate hurdle was not something he wanted to experience again. Atlético Madrid's Europa League success over Marseille had offered him both solace and hope that 2018 would be a memorable year – and on the eve of the most important game of his life it was clear he intended to ensure it.

In Moscow's Luzhniki Stadium, only Croatia stood between France and the 18 carat gold World Cup trophy which, in the event of victory, would enable them to display the sought-after second star on their shirt.

Their road to Russia had not been especially rocky, but Antoine had noticed that, since France's last international tournament, he had become something of a marked man. "I could see that my perspective had changed and that opponents were no longer looking at me in the same way. My performance with *Les Bleus* were analysed more, my team-mates gave me more of the ball. I had become enemy number one for the opposing side. As a result I had someone following me all the time in every game! That was something new, but it prompted me to improve in order that I could continue to hurt teams even when I had someone on my back."

The French, like Griezmann himself, grew into the Russia tournament. They opened their Group C fixtures against Australia in Kazan, Antoine earning – and scoring from – a penalty after he had been tripped in the second half. Although Australia levelled from the spot, France secured the win with an own goal 10 minutes from time.

"It was laborious and we didn't do well," he admitted after being substituted before the hour. "We were not good enough with the ball. It was only the second time I've played up front with Kylian (Mbappé) and Ousmane (Dembélé). We need more time to get used to playing with one another. But I am not worried. It was the first game in a World Cup and it is always special. There is a lot of pressure, especially for the new players. We want to do better in the next game against Peru, which will be tougher."

He was right. The Peruvians put up a spirited display in Yekaturinburg and were only defeated by a first half goal from teenage striking sensation Mbappé. Nevertheless, this win maintained France's lead at the top of the table, thereby offering them safe passage into the round of 16. It is ironic that their final group game, a drab goalless affair against Denmark, should take place in the arena where they would enjoy their greatest success. It was the competition's first 0-0 draw, and the crowd didn't take kindly to it. "We're used to that," Griezmann commented in Moscow. "If you don't score you're going to get whistled. If you don't play well you're going to get whistled. It's up to us to stay cool." Antoine acknowledged that he hadn't yet reached top form, but promised more in the knock-out stages. "The preparation was a bit tough, but I'll keep improving and raising my level of play. I have faith in my game."

It was in the match against Argentina that France began to show what they were capable of. Less than ten minutes had gone in Kazan when Griezmann curled a free-kick against the crossbar, and in the 13th minute the Atlético forward put his team ahead with a penalty after Mbappé had been fouled. Shortly after half-time, Argentina turned the game on its head through Ángel Di María and Gabriel Mercado, before Benjamin Pavard's sizzler and Mbappé's quick-fire double put Didier Deschamps' men so far ahead that Sergio Agüero's reply was insufficient.

"We knew how to stay together in the difficult periods," Antoine said. "We know that a lot of French people are watching us and are expecting great things from us. You want to see Kylian like that on the field. He made the difference by winning the penalty and by scoring two goals. He did brilliantly for us. There are some games when you don't play well, like the one against Denmark, and there are others which are better, like today's. We've got a great team which is going to be hard to beat."

The western Russian city of Nizhny Novgorod played host to France's quarter-final clash, one which was of particular interest to Griezmann for it was against Uruguay, the country with whom he identifies himself. Its culture, values, mentality, music and the food have made such a massive impression on him, not least through his association with Martin Lasarte, the Uruguayan who gave him his debut for Real Sociedad, plus his then team-mate Carlos Bueno and his Atlético colleague Diego Godín, who is godfather to Antoine's daughter Mia.

"Godín made me want to sign for Atlético. He is my best friend. We are always together, in training or away from football. It is going to be a very emotional game for me. It is harder to play against a friend because he knows everything about me, like I know everything about him and (José) Giménez, who also plays with us at Atlético Madrid. Uruguay will be like Atlético. They will take their time, fall down, go to the referee. We will have to get used to that because the match will be boring and they will want to bring us into that."

Antoine marked the occasion with a unique pair of boots. "A special pair for a special match for me," he posted on Twitter as he published a photo of his footwear, with one boot featuring a maté decked in the colours of the French flag and the other the Uruguayan flag.

With their opponents deprived of injured marksman Edinson Cavani, France opened the scoring through Raphaël Varane, who glanced home a header from Griezmann's pin-point free-kick. A semi-final place was sealed in the second half when Antoine's left foot drive squirmed through the hands of keeper Fernando Muslera, earning him congratulations on Instagram from his idol, David Beckham.

However, as pleased as he was to fire his team into the last four and be named Man-of-the-Match, he explained why he didn't celebrate his goal. "It was a Uruguayan who helped me take my first steps in the professional world. I also had a lot of friends on the other side. Out of respect I thought it was natural not to celebrate. We are very happy. Our aim is to go all the way. There are two matches left and we'll see if we can do it. We're going to concentrate on our game and we'll recover well today and over the next three days. There was a bit more pressure on us at the Euros because it was in France and we knew how well we were doing and what the repercussions were. Here, we are in our bubble. We will only take stock of everything at the end of the competition. I began timidly, especially with the ball, but I feel better and better. These are the kind of games I adore."

Griezmann also played a significant part in the hard-fought semi-final win over much-fancied Belgium in Saint Petersburg. It was from his right wing corner that Samuel Umtiti rose to flick home the only goal of the game and set up a Moscow final against Croatia. And in a press conference before the big day, Antoine was in a confident and determined mood. "You should be proud to be French," he declared. "People don't say that often enough. You live well in France, you eat well, we have a beautiful country, we have a good France team, we have beautiful French people, beautiful journalists! I want young people to say: *Vive la France, Vive la République* and be proud they're French. We see pictures, videos and photos. My town of Mâcon went crazy when we got to the final. We hope to make the French people happy. We have confidence in ourselves and I'm sure we'll play a great game. It will be difficult, of course, but we have the potential to do something great and I hope we'll be able to bring the cup home."

The World Cup final proved to be a fitting end to a fabulous tournament, with Antoine again playing a pivotal role in

France's success on July 15th, 2018, Mario Mandžukić inadvertently nodding his curling free-kick into his own net to give the French an 18th minute lead. And although Ivan Perišić equalised, Griezmann's coolly-taken penalty brought his team a half-time lead, which he celebrated with a Fortnite jig, his right hand placed on his forehead and his finger and thumb positioned into an L sign, which in Fortnite language means *take the loss*. Paul Pogba and Kylian Mbappé extended France's advantage before Mandžukić reduced the arrears but, just as he had hoped, Antoine was able to celebrate his most successful of years.

"It was just what I was looking for, what I needed and what I play for: to win trophies," he said, admitting that it took time to appreciate his achievement in Russia.

"You don't realise it because it just doesn't stop. You're playing and training the whole time ... the UEFA Super Cup, La Liga and now we've got the national team again. It's the little things that make it sink in, like the second star on the France shirt, but otherwise ... I didn't take it in.

"There were no words, just lots of emotion. You don't know where to look, whether you should go to your supporters or your family or your team-mates. You do a bit of everything and anything. When you get in the dressing rook it's mad. Everyone wants a photo with the trophy. When you pose for five minutes you realise: 'Fuck, I've done it! We've done it!' You look around you and you see your team-mates going crazy with the cup. Everyone wants to get hold of it. It's incredible.

"We had a bit of luck. You always need a bit of luck if you're going to win, and then there was the fact that we had a different team than at the Euros. I'm not going to lie. At the Euros we thought it was already done. We told ourselves that we had won already after beating Germany. That was the real final for us. We had more attacking power at the World Cup and we were a much more difficult team to break down. Some new players arrived and that was really good for us. They brought added value to our teams. We are a whole squad, who lived together from the start. The substitutes were never in a mood, never annoyed. We've been working for the collective so everything would go well for us. The coach was right. He knew how to analyse matches. I'm really proud of this team."

Despite France's success, they were criticised for winning the World Cup with a style of play which wasn't based on possession. However, Griezmann insisted they won because they played to their strengths.

"The fault for all that lies with (Pep) Guardiola and his Barcelona side!" he joked. "Everyone wanted to play tiki-taka with a 4-3-3 because they won the lot. But you have to have the players to do that and a philosophy focused on that style of play, like Barça, who worked on it with their young players in the academy. In France it's the type of football we played at the World Cup which works for us and it's the same with Atléti. We're not going to change."

It is not solely his international performances which made Antoine the most Googled sportsman in France in 2018. His displays at club level have also contributed to his immense popularity. Despite regular rumours of a move away from Atlético Madrid – he extended his contract by 12 months in June 2017 amid reports of strong Manchester United interest – his loyalty was rewarded with a double trophy haul the following year.

First up was the Europa League, a competition where he scored in every round, including in the semi-final away leg against Arsenal. In the final, against Marseille in Lyon, he broke new ground by becoming the first French player to score twice in a European club final.

He struck first in the 21st minute with a well-placed left foot shot, running to the touchline to perform his Fortnite dance. He doubled Atlético's lead after the break with a deft finish, taking his total to 29 goals in all competitions, before Gabí put the match beyond doubt a minute from time. With Barcelona reported to be willing to pay his 100m euros release clause, many believed this would be Griezmann's final appearance for *Los Colchoneros.*

"I don't think now is the time to talk about my future," he said afterwards. "I want to enjoy the present. I want to enjoy this with the fans."

But in June 2018, to the surprise of many, Antoine announced in a video that he had signed another contract extension at Atlético until 2023, proclaiming on social media: "My fans, my team, MY HOME!!!!" in Spanish, French and English. "Hard to refuse Barça? It was difficult," he admitted. "You have Barça who want you, who call you, who send messages. But then there is the club where you are, where you are an important player and where they build a project around you. What tipped the scales? To see my team-mates, especially the coach, after a game where I was whistled, calm me down and talk with me and show that I had his confidence."

It was suggested that being second choice to Lionel Messi may also have influenced his decision. "Subconsciously being Messi's lieutenant may have played a part. But my team-mates and the people at my club did everything. They came to talk to me, increased my salary. They did everything to show that it was my house and that I shouldn't leave. It was really complicated at times, especially for my wife when I'd wake her up at 3am to talk about it."

Griezmann's European exploits earned him the Europa League Player of the season accolade, making him the second Frenchman to win the award after Paul Pogba's nomination in the previous year. The jury was composed of the coaches from the 48 clubs which participated in the group stage, together with 55 journalists selected by the European Sports Media (ESM) group. The final result was based on the total number of votes cast.

"I am very honoured and proud to receive this award and would like to thank all those who voted for me," he said in a video message. "In particular, I would like to pay special tribute to my coach, to the coaching and medical staff and, of course, to my team-mates. This award is also for the supporters. I am delighted to have won this accolade and I hope this trophy will bring further success, either at a collective or on an individual level."

Griezmann's second trophy of the year with Atlético arrived on August 15th in Tallinn, where city rivals Real Madrid, the current Champions League holders, were defeated 4-2 after extra-time. That success not only prompted him to commission special customised Atléti 'Superbowl'-style rings for his team, it also convinced him he had made the right choice in committing his future to the club.

"I stayed because there was a good project. I have confidence in this club, in *Cholo* (Diego Simeone). Today I saw that I was not wrong. It was time for us to win the Super Cup again. It was very important to start the season like this. I left home because I wanted to win trophies. This is my second and I hope I can win more. This is a reward for all the work I have put in, the suffering. There has been joy and sadness, but I am so happy and I hope to be able to live moments like this again."

It wasn't just Griezmann's professional life which was rewarding. In October 2018, he announced through a video on his Twitter account that he and Erika, whom he had married 16 months earlier, were expecting their second child. Antoine is filmed in his garden chipping a ball towards a target placed between two question marks, one in pink, the other in blue, symbolising the gender of the unborn baby.

Once the target was hit a mechanism released a multitude of blue balloons from a box below. If that didn't serve as a big enough hint that the new arrival will be a boy, then his Twitter message may well have: "See you soon, little prince."

A second child to accompany that second star: on top of the world.

Postscript

OUR ANTOINE

Dad Alain Griezmann and Éric Olhats are the two men in Antoine Griezmann's life. The ones who educated him, shaped him, built him. The ones who know his innermost feelings. This is what they say…

AG: I love all sports but I adore football and I still continue to attend games in Mâcon. Sometimes when I drive past a stadium I'll stop and watch a game in progress. I passed this passion on to Antoine. It's not necessarily hereditary: it's certainly not Maud's world and while Théo is a fan – he plays number 9 for Sporting Mâcon – he doesn't have the same fervour his brother had at that age. I played as a defender, up to fourth division level. I coached youngsters, and still do, because I enjoy getting my messages across.

I look after the town's Under-13s three times a week. Thirteen years, the age Antoine had when I coached him before he left for Real Sociedad. He was my best player. He could run all day. He was the best performer every weekend. But I never paid him a compliment. When he got back home he'd complain to his mum because, as a matter of course, I didn't think he was good enough. I didn't want the people on the sidelines to think that Antoine was only playing because he was the coach's son! I didn't congratulate him much in public, just in private. Even today when he has a great game I don't tell him he was amazing. You've always got to take a look at yourself in football. All the time, all the time. In football, you always have to. It's the basic thing to do at that level.

ÉO: I am Antoine's sports adviser, which means everything and nothing. We get on really well. But it doesn't stop us from saying things and arguing if we have to. I have my personality and I'm blunt. Our relationship, which mixes professionalism with friendship, while based on trust and goodwill, is on an unusual scale. I've got loads of anecdotes about Antoine. But our relationship is based on much more than anecdotes.

From the age of thirteen-and-a-half, when I brought him with me to Bayonne after he had been turned down everywhere, to eighteen-and-a-half we almost lived 365 days a year together, except for the holidays!

He built himself up with me. It was a moral, educational and sporting build-up. I was the prop, the friend, the Père Fouettard, the uncle, the grandfather and Santa Claus all at once. I suffered for him, with him. I was neither prepared nor ready to welcome and live with a boy to whom I would be so attached.

I had to be accountable to his parents, sometimes having the impression that in their eyes I had kidnapped him! Initially they didn't really like him being at my house. I hadn't intended to put him up but it was better. If I'd put him in a boarding school in Spain, where he didn't speak the language, he'd have hitchhiked straight back. Yes, he cried at my place when he missed his family, to whom he is extremely close. Neither they nor he realised the upheavals which would occur. When he returned to Bayonne after a weekend in Mâcon, his father had tears in his eyes, his mother would hide away and he wasn't good in himself. I made him work at school and I paid his air fare so he could go back home. On the weekends that he stayed I would take him to games in Toulouse or Bordeaux, which I'd be watching for Real Sociedad. Even though he is not my son, I shared his joys and his sorrows.

AG: I watch all his games, really all of them. I can't have missed many of them. Even when Real Sociedad were playing in the second division I would find a way of following them on the Internet. Let's say I watch them with intensity … However, I prefer to be alone. I can't watch one of his games with anyone because everyone will have their own point of view and it won't be the same as mine. I need to be alone even when my wife and my son are in the house. I look at everything in detail, I get angry, I smile, I get carried away and I get annoyed when he makes a bad pass. I express my joy when he scores. I don't call him after every game but I do so often. He has moved to another level since he's been at Atlético. Diego Simeone asks a lot of him. With him, if you don't defend you don't play. You either embrace it or you don't … I watched a training session and it was a real treat. When I see his team play I fixate on Antoine. I don't pay too much attention to his team-mates.

ÉO: It was at a tournament in Saint-Germain-en-Laye, when he was having a trial with Montpellier that I spotted him, and then I brought him with me to the Basque Country. When he began to get star billing it was as if I was a magician, someone who saw what nobody else had seen before. This needs to be tempered. I am not the hero who discovered Antoine. I was working in Spain, where his size was more sought after than in the French developmental system. Technically he was very adept, which is what made the difference. At the time Antoine was cut like a Smurf!

I soon knew that his trial with Real Sociedad would be conclusive. I don't consider myself a magician, nor, as it happens a ruthless meat trader who would put the sporting aspect ahead of human values. I have spent some marvellous moments with him, where we've had lots of genuine laughter and a great connection.

His loyalty brings me a kind of recognition and doubtless enhances my status. But our story is a life story. The reason I'm still at his side today is because he considers me someone important. Not a day goes by when we don't talk to each other. We always talk when there's a game, both before and after. We use WhatsApp rather than the conventional phone calls. Whenever his performance hasn't been out of the ordinary, I'm one of the few people, with his father, who is able to tell him why. Antoine, who is very demanding of himself, can take it from me. He needs someone who's going to tell him if he has been rubbish or not.

AG: Antoine always wanted to follow me when I was coaching. He would find his friends and would play football next to our games. He didn't watch them and he would ask me the score at the end. When we were on holiday in the South of France in the summer of 1997, we took in Monaco/Châteauroux at the Stade Louis II. Facing the team which was newly-promoted to

Ligue 1 were Fabien Barthez, Ali Benarbia, David Trezeguet and Thierry Henry. There was a sparse crowd and Antoine was the only one not following the game: he was playing with his ball! He was juggling, enjoying himself and wasn't interested in what was happening in the game.

Later, in Lyon's Stade Gerland, he enjoyed the atmosphere and the occasion. Lyon didn't take him on. He had so many trials which weren't conclusive. The last straw came with Metz's refusal. That hurt Antoine. He was bad, very bad.

When Lens then called me I said: "No, we're stopping all this!" Then Éric Olhats spotted him in a tournament. We were on holiday with his mum. Antoine had left his business card on the fridge, insisting I contacted him as soon as we got back. I thought it was a joke. I didn't want him to be disappointed again. Antoine badgered me so much that I replied: "Right, OK. I'm going to call him in front of you."

Éric suggested he spent a week on trial at Real Sociedad. I didn't jump for joy because I was still suspicious. To prove to me how determined he was, Éric said: "I'm coming to Mâcon." We were 800 kilometres from his home in Bayonne. "Do what you want," I replied.

I didn't take this too seriously. But on the Monday he was in Mâcon. We met up in a hotel in the north of the town. He repeated his offer of a week's trial, at the club's expense. I didn't say "yes" straight away. I checked him out and I understood that he was someone I could trust."

ÉO: We've been through so much together in this daunting football world ... Antoine is a paradoxical boy. Underneath his shy appearance he knows exactly what he wants. He also knows how to be selfish when he needs to be, as his profession demands. He is an epicurean. He's a big eater and he devours life. He also has an atypical, refreshing and humble personality.

His parents and I got involved after his road trip with the France Under-21 team, which resulted in a 13 month ban at all international levels. We had to make him understand that what he had done was serious, but also that no-one had died. It was one of those "aha!" moments, a realisation. Antoine had been afraid. Perhaps he'd thought he was untouchable. Through this episode, which even Les Guignols de l'Info *(1)* used, he lost his boyish innocence. He screwed up, but it was important that we deployed some psychology and teaching instruction. Getting stuck into him would serve no purpose. Antoine is an emotional person, who goes into his shell if you harp on too much. He's the kind of guy who can side-step problems. His big maxim is this: "I don't want to complicate things." He lives for today. And he's always got a smile on his face.

AG: It was difficult letting him leave on his own. As parents we asked ourselves questions. My wife, a real mother hen, was afraid at him being so far away and she wanted to protect him. Me, I encouraged him: "Go, son. So many clubs have shut their door on you. You have never had this opportunity. At least you'll have tried. I dreamed of becoming professional. It's a chance of a lifetime. If you're not happy, you come back."

He lived at Éric's house. At that time there weren't many mobile phones around. We would go on all our holidays by car – the plane was too expensive – so we could visit him. When I took him to the airport on a Sunday evening, after a weekend in Mâcon, my wife preferred not to come because it would tear her apart. I heard Antoine crying on the back seat. "So do we stop or what? It's no problem if you want to go back home."

The choice was his. We didn't have a contract, just his playing licence. But Antoine was determined. "No, Dad, I can do it," he said. And we carried on.

Real Sociedad turned out to be the ideal club, with deep values. He learned everything down there. Éric and I have strong personalities. There were a few justified moments of friction but they were always respectful.

We both took care of Antoine. Me on the financial and administrative side, and him when it came to football. When news came out about the five Under-21 players' trip to Paris, I guessed Antoine was mixed up in it. I reckoned he was frustrated about not playing. It was a stupid thing to do but he paid the price. It was much easier to have a go at five youngsters than the people who have made really big mistakes. We called a crisis meeting with Éric. We got Antoine re-focused and he took responsibility for that nonsense.

It served as a lesson for him because he became a new man afterwards. But he remains like me: solid.

ÉO: I am part of his life, a life which is out of the ordinary, both for him and for me. Its intensity reached a crescendo from the frozen ready meals to the talks with the world's biggest clubs!

I have always been immersed in football, and our closeness has enabled him to avoid certain traps. A qualified national sports instructor from the age of 20, I had responsibilities very early on. I was in charge of the academy at Pau, the technical boss of Aviron Bayonnais – me, a pure Basque – and I worked on the development side at Toulouse, Bastia and Sochaux.

I have worked with Real Sociedad since 2003, for whom I am one of the scouts at professional level. I spend 250 days a year outside Europe, scouring tournaments in Brazil, Singapore,

Canada or New Zealand. I love my freedom. I live it to the full.

I have also been a council employee for sport in Bayonne and I had a shot at an experience in England with the British company ISM (International Sports Management). I was based in Birmingham, where I had to accompany and discover future pros for the English league by spotting them in Europe and Africa. This company of agents wasn't my thing.

And I came back to Real Sociedad, for whom I am always on the road. I love my job. Antoine asked me to look after him when I was on my way back from Birmingham. It wasn't easy being judge and jury, but this break had done us good. We had cut the umbilical cord! He'd needed to break free and I, too, needed to find some form of freedom again. I enjoyed our reunion.

We are like magnets: we draw each other together and, even if we have been apart, we always end up at the starting point!

AG: The family took in all the games of the Euros (in 2016). Antoine went up a scale and took on a new dimension. I suffered during those two lost finals, in the Champions League and the Euros. It's a pity things didn't finish in a blaze of glory. But that's the appeal of football: the best don't necessarily win. I am proud of how it has all panned out for him. There is no feeling of vindictiveness.

The Antoine Griezmann Challenge, which we organise in Mâcon, is a way of pleasing the town and the kids. There are about 40 members of *Team Grizi*, of which I'm the president, and we are all volunteers. Over one weekend almost 800 children from nine to 13 play in the tournaments and 5,000 people pass through.

I work for my son. Even though Antoine is a star he is still my lad. I don't worship in front of him. If I want to yell at him and push him around I'm fine with that.

I'll soon be 60, and I'm still working for the town of Mâcon because I want to earn my retirement! We have three children and we have made sure we show no favouritism. There is no jealousy between brothers and sister. They know how to get on with each other. And the reason why a lot of the family meals revolve around Antoine is because we are all football lovers!

(1) France's equivalent of Spitting Image.

AG: Stats

Born: March 21st, 1991.
Place Of Birth: Mâcon, France.
Age: 28.
Nationality: French .

CLUB CAREER

Appearances (Subs)/Goals

Real Sociedad
July 1st, 2009 –
August 17th, 2014

League:
132 (17)/40
Cup:
6 (0)/0

Atlético Madrid
August 17th, 2014
– Current

League:
161 (12)/92
Cup:
67 (10)/39

Total career (League)
293 (29)/132
Total career (Cup)
73 (10)/39

Overall club career total
366 (39)/171

Goal per game average
(League): 0.45
Goal per game average
(Cup): 0.53

INTERNATIONAL CAREER

Appearances/Goals: 69/28
Youth debut: March 2, 2010
Senior debut: March 5,
2014 v Netherlands
First goal: June 1, 2014
v Paraguay

Season by season

(All club games and internationals)

2018/2019

Appearances: 49
Goals: 23
Yellow cards: 10
Red cards: 0

2017/2018

Appearances: 63
Goals: 36
Yellow cards: 9
Red cards: 1

2016/2017

Appearances: 59
Goals: 28
Yellow cards: 4
Red cards: 0

2015/2016

Appearances: 68
Goals: 40
Yellow cards: 6
Red cards: 0

2014/2015

Appearances: 56
Goals: 25
Yellow cards: 10
Red cards: 0

2013/2014

Appearances: 45
Goals: 16
Yellow cards: 5
Red cards: 0

2012/2013

Appearances: 34
Goals: 10
Yellow cards: 8
Red cards: 0

2011/2012

Appearances: 35
Goals: 7
Yellow cards: 5
Red cards: 0

Continued over

ANTOINE GRIEZMANN

2010/2011

Appearances: 37
Goals: 7
Yellow cards: 6
Red cards: 0

2009/2010

Appearances: 8
Goals: 0
Yellow cards: 2
Red cards: 0

International tournaments

World Cup

2014 (Brazil):
Appearances: 4
Goals: 0

2018 (Russia):
Appearances: 7
Goals: 4

European Championships

2016 (France):
Appearances: 7
Goals: 6

Honours

Real Sociedad:

Spanish Second Division 2009–10

Atlético Madrid:

Spanish Supercup 2014
UEFA Europa League 2018
UEFA Super Cup 2018

France:

UEFA Under-19 Championships 2010
FIFA World Cup 2018

Personal:

Ballon d'Or 2016, 2018 – 3rd
La Liga Player of the Year 2016
UEFA European Championship Player of the Tournament & Golden Boot 2016
FIFA World Cup Bronze Ball & Silver Boot 2018

Stats up to 03/04/19. Source: Soccerbase.com

The players in France's 2018 football team which won the World Cup were awarded the Legion of Honour in the 2019 new year's honours list.

The 23 players, including Antoine Griezmann, each received France's top medal for their part in beating Croatia in the World Cup final in Moscow.

The Legion of Honour is the highest French order of merit for military and civil merits, established in 1802 by Napoleon Bonaparte.

THANKS...

I would first like to thank my parents for bringing me into the world and for instilling such good values into me, ones which today, in turn, I pass on to my daughter Mia.

Thank you Dad for introducing me to football. I am thrilled to be able to live your dream!

Thank you Mum for still showing me the same love today as you have done ever since my birth. You are always taking care of me and I am really touched by your attention.

Thank you Maud for managing my diary between the sponsors and the press, for putting up with my bad temper and for putting a smile back on my face every time you visit Madrid with the macaroons which you have brought directly from Paris.

Thank you Théo for being that ball of energy which makes me laugh all the time. I am very proud of you and of what you are undertaking with the GZ brand.

Gracias Erika. Without you I wouldn't be the man and the player that I am today! There is a before and an after the day we met. You give me everything I need: love, a smile, the strength … you are my star. You gave me the most beautiful present with our little girl. I am very proud to be the husband of Erika Choperena Aldanondo.

Thank you to you, Éric, my sporting adviser, but most of all, my friend. You gave me the chance to grow in a professional club without ever taking a wrong turning on our road together and you helped me overcome my moments of doubt.

A thousand thank yous go to Martin Lasarte, Philippe Montanier, Cholo Simeone and Didier Deschamps for letting me learn at your sides. Each of you has been vitally important at one period of my career and I will be forever grateful to you.

Thank you Arnaud for following me on this wonderful journey by helping me write this book. Your calmness and your kindness allowed me to produce it more easily and, you've got to say, it was a bit of a long shot!

Thank you also to the Laffont team: Charlotte, Emmanuelle, Bernadette, Lydie, Cécile, Roman, Françoise, Claire, Joël, Astrid, Pascaline, Barbara, Maud, Monique, Alice and all the others.

And finally a big thank you to *Team Grizi*, who are always there to support me with photos, videos or comments on social media. Unfortunately I'm not able to reply to all of you, but you know that I am aware of all your encouragement, with the help of my friend and community manager, André.

Antoine

Antoine Griezmann:
The Making Of A Legend

With heart and determination, Antoine Griezmann overcame his small stature to become one of the world's top soccer players and a World Cup champion.

Released on Netflix March 21st, 2019

For more information about Reach Sport log on to

www.reachsport.com

Reach Sport